D1539765

SWITZERLAND

SCHWEIZ • SUISSE • SVIZZERA • SVIZRA

Zürichberg-Verlag

© 1994 Zürichberg-Verlag C. Locher, 8044 Zürich

Fotos: Siegfried Eigstler, Herbert Haltmeier,
Arnold Odermatt, Lisa Gensetter, Hanspeter Reinhard,
Sigi Stangier, Jacques Straesslé, Christian Thoma
Text: Martin Sigrist, Cyrill Gartmann
Fotolithos: Color-Print AG, Zürich
Druck: A. Hug & Co. AG, Arbon
Papier: Sihl & Eika Papier AG
Bindung: Benziger AG, Einsiedeln

Gedruckt auf Ikonofix chlorfrei 170 gm2 der
ZANDERS Feinpapiere AG

Printed in Switzerland
ISBN 3-9520092-0-2

Inhalt
Table de matières
Indice
Contents

Die Schweiz

Mitten in Europa liegt ein kleines Land, dessen landschaftliche Schönheit in der ganzen Welt bekannt ist: die Schweiz. Die Vielfalt der Gegenden reicht von den mit ewigem Schnee bedeckten Hochalpen bis zum mediterran beeinflussten Tessin - und das alles auf kleinstem Raum. Kein Wunder, ist die Schweiz ein vielbesuchtes Ferienland.

Am 1. August 1291 als Urschweizer Bund auf dem Rütli am Vierwaldstättersee gegründet, feierte die Schweiz 1991 ihr 700jähriges Bestehen. Dass die demokratische Tradition des Landes 1848 in der Gründung des Bundesstaates ihren definitiven Niederschlag gefunden und bis heute erhalten hat, ist sicher keine Selbstverständlichkeit, denn so vielfältig wie die Landschaften sind auch die Kulturen der Deutschschweiz, der Westschweiz, des Tessins und von Romanisch Graubünden.

Heute steht die Schweizer Bevölkerung vor der nicht einfachen Aufgabe, die Schönheit dieses einmaligen Fleckchens Erde auch für kommende Generationen zu erhalten.

La Suisse

Au cœur de l'Europe se situe un petit pays célèbre dans le monde entier par la beauté de ses paysages: la Suisse. La richesse de ses visages passe des neiges éternelles des cimes des Alpes aux allures méditerranéennes du Tessin - le tout sur un espace très restreint. Rien d'étonnant donc à la fascination touristique exercée par ce pays.

La Suisse, dont la fondation remonte à l'alliance perpétuelle conclue le 1er août 1291 par les premiers Confédérés sur le Rütli au bord du lac des Quatre-Cantons, célébra en 1991 son 700ème anniversaire. La tradition démocratique du pays, définitivement concrétisée en 1848 par la fondation de l'Etat fédéral et qui s'est maintenue jusqu'à nos jours, n'allait certainement pas de soi, tant il est vrai que les cultures de la Suisse alémanique, de la Romandie, du Tessin et des Grisons romanches sont aussi différentes que les paysages eux-mêmes.

Aujourd'hui, la population est confrontée au défi délicat de préserver ce coin de terre unique pour les générations futures.

La Svizzera

Nel centro dell'Europa c'è una piccola nazione, i cui paesaggi sono noti in tutto il mondo per la loro bellezza: è la Svizzera. Il panorama varia dalle vette alpine ricoperte dalle nevi eterne fino al Ticino, con il suo carattere tipicamente mediterraneo - e il tutto in uno spazio ridottissimo. Non c'è nulla da meravigliarsi quindi, se la Svizzera è molto apprezzata dai turisti.

Sorta dal patto che i primi confederati stabilirono il 1° agosto 1291 sul Rütli, in riva al Lago dei Quattro Cantoni, la Svizzera ha festeggiato nel 1991 i suoi 700 anni di esistenza. Il fatto che la tradizione democratica del paese abbia trovato la sua base definitiva nella Confederazione del 1848 e abbia potuto mantenersi fino ad oggi, non è cosa certo ovvia, dato che le culture della Svizzera tedesca, della Svizzera francese, del Ticino e del Grigioni romancio sono altrettanto variate quanto i loro paesaggi.

Oggigiorno il popolo svizzero si trova davanti al difficile compito di conservare anche per le future generazioni la bellezza di questa eccezionale zolla di terra.

Switzerland

In the middle of Europe lies a small country whose landscapes are known for their beauty all over the world: Switzerland. The variety of the scenery ranges from the high Alps draped in eternal snows to the Mediterranean-seeming luxuriance of the Ticino - and all within a very small compass. It can surprise no one that Switzerland is a much-visited holiday country.

Founded on 1 August 1291, when the Central Swiss swore an oath of alliance in the Rütli meadow beside the Lake of Uri, Switzerland celebrated its 700th anniversary in 1991. The country's democratic traditions were given their firm embodiment with the founding, in 1848, of a federal state which has continued essentially unchanged to the present. This was not something that could have been taken for granted, for the cultures of German and French Switzerland, the Ticino and the Romanic Grisons are as diverse as the country's landscapes.

Today the people of Switzerland face the not so simple task of preserving the beauty of this unique corner of the earth for future generations.

Bern · Berne · Berna

1

2

3

4

5

Die Stadt **Bern** wurde im 12. Jhdt. von den Zähringern gegründet. Seit 1848 ist sie Bundeshauptstadt der Schweiz. Das Bundeshaus, Sitz von Parlament und Regierung, ist am oberen Bildrand zu erkennen.

Die weitgehend intakte **Berner Altstadt** mit ihren typischen Längsgassen wird von der Aare umflossen. Das spätgotische Münster St. Vincenz (Bildmitte) ist eines der Wahrzeichen der "Bärenstadt".

Weltweit bekannt geworden ist das **Emmental** dank dem gleichnamigen Hartkäse mit den typischen Löchern. Über den Weilern beim Dorf Biglen erhebt sich das Panorama der Berner Alpenkette.

Über Erlach am Bielersee mit dem Schloss aus dem 11. Jhdt. geht der Blick zur **St. Petersinsel**. Mit der Regulierung des Flusses Aare im Jahre 1878 wurde sie zu einer Halbinsel; heute steht sie unter Naturschutz.

Twann, reizvolles Rebbauerndorf an den Gestaden des Bielersees und Herkunftsort eines beliebten Weissweines (Twanner). Die spätgotische reformierte Kirche St. Martin wurde im 17. Jhdt. barock umgebaut.

La ville de **Berne** a été fondée au 12ème siècle par les Zähringer. Elle est la capitale de la Confédération depuis 1848. En haut, le Palais fédéral, siège du Parlement et du gouvernement.

La **vieille ville de Berne**, presque intégralement conservée avec ses typiques ruelles en longueur, est entourée par l'Aar. La cathédrale St. Vincenz de la fin de l'époque gothique (au centre) est l'un des symboles de la "ville des ours".

L'**Emmental** est devenu mondialement célèbre grâce à son fromage à pâte dure du même nom dont les trous sont légendaires. Le panorama de la chaîne bernoise des Alpes se dresse au-dessus des hameaux vers le village de Biglen.

Au-dessus d'Erlach au bord du lac de Bienne, avec son château du 11ème siècle, le regard s'étire jusqu'à l'**Ile St-Pierre**. Suite à la canalisation de l'Aar en 1878, cette île s'est transformée en presqu'île; aujourd'hui, c'est une zone protégée.

Twann, charmant village viticole sur les rives du lac de Bienne et berceau d'un vin blanc très apprécié (Twanner). L'église réformée de St. Martin, gothique tardif, a été transformée dans l'esprit baroque au 17ème siècle.

La città di **Berna** venne fondata nell'11. sec. dagli Zähringer. Dal 1848 è la capitale della Svizzera. Il Palazzo Federale, sede del parlamento e del governo, è ben visibile in alto nella foto.

La **città vecchia**, con le sue tipiche stradine, è rimasta praticamente intatta. Viene bagnata dall'Aare. La cattedrale di St. Vincenz, dell'epoca tardo-gotica (al centro della foto), è uno dei monumenti più caratteristici della "città degli orsi".

La fama mondiale dell'**Emmental** è certamente dovuta all'omonimo formaggio a pasta dura, con i tipici buchi. Sullo sfondo dei caseggiati sparsi del paese di Biglen, si innalzano le Alpi bernesi.

Da Erlach, sulle rive del Lago di Bienna, dal castello dell'11. secolo, lo sguardo spazia fino alla **St. Petersinsel**. A causa delle opere realizzate per regolare il deflusso dell'Aare, nel 1878 divenne una penisola; oggigiorno è una zona protetta.

Twann è un grazioso villaggio situato sulle sponde del Lago di Bienna, al centro di una nota zona viticola. Produce un apprezzato vino bianco (Twanner). La chiesa protestante di St. Martin risale all'epoca tardo-gotica, ma nel 17. sec. venne trasformata in stile barocco.

The city of **Berne** was founded in the 12th century by the Zähringer dynasty. It has been the federal capital of Switzerland since 1848. The Federal Palace, seat of the parliament and government, can be seen right of centre at the top of this picture.

The **Old Town**, preserved almost intact with its typical longitudinal streets, is enclosed by a loop of the River Aare. The Late Gothic minster, St. Vincent's (top centre), is one of the landmarks of the "town of bears".

The **Emmental**, valley of the River Emme, has made a name all over the world because of its cheese, unmistakably characterized by its holes. The panorama of the Bernese Alps here forms a frieze beyond the village of Biglen and other hamlets.

From the slopes above Erlach on the Lake of Bienne, with its eleventh-century castle, there is a good view of the **Ile Saint-Pierre**, St. Peter's Island, now under nature conservancy. Today it is actually a peninsula, for the waters of the lake were lowered by a regulation scheme in 1878.

The charming wine-growing village of **Twann** on the shores of the Lake of Bienne (German Bielersee) produces a popular white wine known as Twanner. The Protestant church of St. Martin's is Late Gothic but was redesigned to suit Baroque tastes in the 17th century.

Berner Oberland · Oberland bernois

1

2

3

4

5

Wie die Stadt Bern wurde auch das **Schloss Thun** im 12. Jhdt. von Zähringer Rittern erbaut. Die vier Ecktürme zeigen Anlehnungen zu normannischen Burgen. Im grossen Wohnturm befinden sich ein prachtvoller Rittersaal und das Historische Museum.

Tout comme la ville de Berne, le **château de Thoune** a lui aussi été construit au 12ème siècle par des chevaliers Zähringer. Les quatres tours d'angle rappellent les forts normans. Actuellement, la grande tour habitable abrite le Musée historique ainsi que la somptueuse salle des chevaliers.

Come la città di Berna, anche il **castello di Thun** venne costruito nel 12. sec. dai cavalieri Zähringer. Le quattro torri ricordano le roccaforti normanne. Nella grande torre abitabile si trovano una magnifica Sala dei Cavalieri e il Museo storico.

Like the city of Berne, **Thun Castle** was built by Zähringer knights in the 12th century. The four angle turrets recall Norman strongholds. The main tower accommodates a splendid great hall and the Historical Museum.

Blick vom **Brienzer Rothorn** (2350 m ü. M.) auf den Brienzersee und das Panorama der Berner Alpen. Von Brienz aus führt eine dampfbetriebene Zahnradbahn aus dem Jahre 1892 aufs Rothorn.

Vue du **Brienzer Rothorn** (2350 m) sur le lac de Brienz avec le panorama des Alpes bernoises. Depuis Brienz, un chemin de fer à crémaillère à vapeur datant de 1892 conduit sur le Rothorn.

Il panorama che si ammira dal **Brienzer Rothorn** (2350 m.s.m.): il Lago di Brienz e le Alpi bernesi. Da Brienz una ferrovia a cremagliera con locomotiva a vapore, risalente al 1892, permette di arrivare fino al Rothorn.

A view from the **Brienzer Rothorn** (2350 metres above sea level) of the Lake of Brienz and the panorama of the Bernese Alps. A steam-powered rack railway line opened in 1892 runs up from Brienz to the top of the Rothorn.

Das Dorf **Brienz** ist bekannt als Zentrum des Berner Oberländer Holzschnitzer-Gewerbes. Beliebte Ausflugsziele in der Region sind das Freilichtmuseum Ballenberg mit historischen Gebäuden aus der ganzen Schweiz, die Giessbach-Fälle sowie das Brienzer Rothorn.

Le village de **Brienz** est fameux comme centre de l'artisanat local, la sculpture sur bois. Le musée en plein air de Ballenberg, avec ses maisons historiques de tout le pays, est un but d'excursion aussi apprécié que les chutes de Giessbach et le Rothorn.

Il paese di **Brienz** è noto per essere il centro dell'intaglio del legno. Le mete più apprezzate per le escursioni nella regione sono il Museo del Ballenberg (museo della civiltà contadina, all'aperto) con edifici storici di tutta la Svizzera, le cascate del Giessbach e il Brienzer Rothorn.

The village of **Brienz** is well known as the centre of the Bernese Oberland's wood carving trade. Popular destinations for excursions in this region are the Ballenberg open-air museum, where historical buildings from all over Switzerland are preserved, the famous Giessbach Falls and the Brienzer Rothorn.

Oberhalb des Kurortes Grindelwald erstreckt sich ein weitläufiges Wandergebiet, das imposante Ausblicke bietet. Vom Dorfrand aus schweift der Blick zum zerklüfteten **Wetterhorn** (3701 m ü. M.).

Un vaste territoire de randonnée s'étend au pied de la station touristique de Grindelwald d'où la vue est majestueuse. Depuis la lisière du village, le regard embrasse le visage fissuré du **Wetterhorn** (3701 mètres).

Sopra alla nota stazione turistica di Grindelwald si estende una vasta regione che offre magnifiche escursioni con panorami imponenti. Dai margini del paese lo sguardo spazia fino al **Wetterhorn** (3701 m.s.m.), con la sua cresta frastagliata.

Above the famous resort of Grindelwald there is an extensive happy hunting ground for hikers and climbers that offers many wonderful views. This one, photographed from the edge of the village, is of the rugged **Wetterhorn** (3701 metres).

Schreckhorn und **Finsteraarhorn** gehören zu den markantesten Gipfeln des Berner Oberlandes. Zwischen ihren Flanken fliesst ein Gletscher talwärts, dessen Zunge nur wenige hundert Meter oberhalb Grindelwald endet.

Le **Schreckhorn** et le **Finsteraarhorn** font partie des sommets les plus marquants de l'Oberland bernois. Entre leurs flancs, un glacier s'écoule vers la vallée dont la langue s'achève quelques centaines de mètres à peine au-dessus de Grindelwald.

Schreckhorn e **Finsteraarhorn** sono fra le vette più imponenti dell'Oberland bernese. Lungo i loro fianchi si snoda fino a valle un ghiacciaio, la cui lingua arriva fino a poche centinaia di metri sopra a Grindelwald.

Two of the most striking peaks in the Bernese Oberland are the **Schreckhorn** and the **Finsteraarhorn**. A glacier flows down between their steep flanks, ending in a snout that is only a few hundred metres above Grindelwald.

1

2

3

4

Unweit von Kandersteg liegt der **Öschinensee**, der mit einem Sessellift und einer kurzen Wanderung bequem zu erreichen ist. Dahinter erhebt sich das vergletscherte Massiv der Blümlisalp (3664 m ü. M.).

Le **lac d'Oeschinen**, confortablement atteignable en télésiège et une courte promenade, est situé à peu de distance de Kandersteg. Derrière lui se dresse le massif de glaciers de la Blümlisalp (3664 m).

A poca distanza da Kandersteg, dopo una rapida ascesa con la seggiovia e una breve passeggiata, si può arrivare comodamente all'**Oeschinensee**. Dietro si erge il massiccio del Blümlisalp, con i suoi ghiacci eterni (3664 m.s.m.)

Not far from Kandersteg lies the **Oeschinensee**, a mountain lake that can be reached comfortably by a short walk from the top of a chair-lift. Behind it rises the glacier-furrowed massif of the Blümlisalp (3664 metres).

Eiger, **Mönch** und **Jungfrau** - eine der wohl berühmtesten Gebirgsgruppen der Welt. Die Nordwand des Eigers (links im Bild), 1938 erstmals bezwungen, zählt auch heute noch zu den anspruchs- und risiko-vollsten bergsteigerischen Unternehmungen in den Alpen.
Die höchste Erhebung des Dreigestirns ist die Jungfrau (rechts) mit 4158 m ü. M. Die beiden anderen Gipfel liegen knapp an der Viertausend-Meter-Grenze.

Eiger, **Mönch** et **Jungfrau** - l'un des groupes de montagnes sans doute parmi les plus fameux du monde. La paroi nord de l'Eiger (à gauche), vaincue pour la première fois en 1938, est aujourd'hui encore considérée comme l'une des ascensions les plus difficiles et les plus dangereuses des Alpes.
La Jungfrau (à droite) culmine à la plus haute altitude dans ce groupe avec 4158 m. Les deux autres sommets se situent juste à la limite des quatre mille.

Eiger, **Mönch** e **Jungfrau** - uno dei massicci montagnosi più conosciuti del mondo. La parete nord dell'Eiger (a sinistra nella foto), conquistata per la prima volta nel 1938, rappresenta ancora oggi una delle imprese alpinistiche più esigenti e più rischiose.
La vetta più alta della triade è la Jungfrau (a destra) che arriva a 4158 m.s.m. Le altre due cime sono appena al limite dei quattromila.

Eiger, **Mönch** and **Jungfrau** form one of the most famous groups of mountains in the world. The North Face of the Eiger (left), first climbed in 1938, is still one of the most demanding and perilous ascents in the Alps.
The highest of the three summits is that of the Jungfrau (right) at 4158 metres. The other two peaks are just at the four-thousand-metre mark.

Eine von 1896 bis 1912 erbaute Bahn führt von der Kleinen Scheidegg durch einen Tunnel von sieben Kilometern Länge aufs **Jungfraujoch** (3475 m). Bergstation, Aussichts-Plattform und das Observatorium auf der Sphinx sind auf dem Bild gut zu erkennen.

Un chemin de fer construit entre 1896 et 1912 conduit de la Petite Scheidegg à travers un tunnel de sept kilomètres vers le **Jungfraujoch** (3475 m). On reconnaît bien sur cette illustration la station d'altitude, la plate-forme panoramique et l'observatoire sur le sphinx.

Una linea ferroviaria, costruita fra il 1896 e il 1912, porta dalla Kleine Scheidegg, attraverso una galleria lunga sette chilometri, fino allo **Jungfraujoch** (3475 m.s.m.). La stazione d'arrivo, la piattaforma panoramica e l'osservatorio sulla "Sphinx" sono chiaramente visibili nella foto.

A railway built between 1896 and 1912 runs from the Kleine Scheidegg through a seven-kilometre-long tunnel on to the saddle of **Jungfraujoch** (3475 metres). The mountain station, the lookout platform and the observatory on top of the Sphinx rock are visible in this picture.

Das Jungfraujoch gehört zu den bekanntesten touristischen Zielen der Schweiz - entsprechend gross ist der Besucherstrom während den Sommermonaten. Der Blick nach Südosten erstreckt sich über den **Jungfraufirn** in Richtung Konkordiaplatz.

La Jungfraujoch est l'une des plus fameuses destinations touristiques de Suisse - l'affluence des visiteurs est donc particulièrement dense pendant les mois d'été. La vue au sud-est s'étend par-dessus le **Jungfraufirn** en direction du Konkordiaplatz.

Lo Jungfraujoch è una delle mete turistiche più conosciute della Svizzera - altrettanto massiccio è il flusso di turisti durante i mesi estivi. Lo sguardo verso sudest può spaziare oltre lo **Jungfraufirn** in direzione di Konkordiaplatz.

Jungfraujoch is one of the most popular tourist destinations in Switzerland, attracting great crowds of sightseers in the summer months. From the top there is a fine southeastern view towards Konkordiaplatz, across the **Jungfraufirn**, whose snow is gradually turning to glacier ice.

Zentralschweiz · Suisse centrale

1

2

3

4

Luzern ist das wirtschaftliche, kulturelle und touristische Zentrum der Innerschweiz. Die Altstadt beidseits der Reuss ist reich an historischen Gebäuden; die Jesuitenkirche (am linken Bildrand) gilt als erster grosser Barockbau der Schweiz. Wahrzeichen der Kantonshauptstadt am Vierwaldstättersee ist die um das Jahr 1300 erbaute Kapellbrücke.

Lucerne est le centre économique, culturel et touristique de la Suisse centrale. La vieille ville, des deux côtés de la Reuss, est riche en bâtiments historiques; l'église des jésuites (en bas à gauche) est considérée comme la première grande construction baroque de Suisse. Le pont couvert en bois, construit vers 1300, est le symbole de ce chef-lieu cantonal au bord du lac des Quatre-Cantons.

Lucerna è il centro economico, culturale e turistico della Svizzera interna. La città vecchia, sulle due sponde della Reuss, è ricca di edifici storici. La Jesuitenkirche (a sinistra, nella foto) viene considerata la prima grande costruzione barocca in Svizzera. Marchio della capitale cantonale, in riva al Lago dei Quattro Cantoni, è il tipico "Kapellbrücke", un ponte costruito intorno al 1300.

Lucerne is the economic, cultural and touristic centre of the core region of Switzerland. The old quarter, on both sides of the River Reuss, has a wealth of historic buildings: the Jesuit Church (far left) was the country's first great Baroque edifice. The Kapellbrücke, or Chapel Bridge, built around 1300, is the best-known gem of this lakeside cantonal capital.

Ein prächtiger Ausblick auf die beiden Felspyramiden der **Mythen** im Kanton Schwyz. Der grosse Mythen (links) lässt sich von geübten Wanderern ohne Seil und Pickel bewältigen, während der kleine Mythen ein nicht ungefährliches Kletterparadies darstellt.

Une superbe perspective sur les deux pyramides rocheuses des **Mythen** dans le canton de Schwyz. Le grand Mythen (à gauche) est à la portée de tous les randonneurs exercés sans corde ni piolet, tandis que le petit Mythen est un paradis de la varappe non sans danger.

Una magnifica veduta delle piramidi di roccia dei due **Mythen**, nel Canton Svitto. Il grande Mythen (a sinistra) può essere conquistato anche da escursionisti ben allenati, senza bisogno di corde né di picozze, mentre il piccolo Mythen rappresenta un vero paradiso per gli alpinisti, peraltro non scevro di pericoli.

A fine view of the two rocky pyramids of the **Mythen** in the Canton of Schwyz. The Greater Mythen (left) can be scaled by trained mountain hikers without ropes or axes, while the Lesser Mythen (right) attracts skilled rock climbers and is not without its dangers.

Der Urnersee bildet das südöstlichste Becken des Vierwaldstättersees. Im Vordergrund links der Kurort Brunnen mit seinen zahlreichen Hotels und der Uferpromenade. Die am felsigen Seeufer zu erkennende Axenstrasse führt in Richtung Altdorf - Gotthard.

L'Urnersee forme l'extrémité sud-est du lac des Quatre-Cantons; au premier plan à gauche, la station de Brunnen avec ses nombreux hôtels et sa promenade. Le grand axe qu'on reconnaît sur la rive rocheuse du lac conduit en direction d'Altdorf - Gothard.

Il Lago di Uri è in realtà il bacino sud-orientale del Lago dei Quattro Cantoni. A sinistra si nota Brunnen, nota stazione climatica, con i suoi numerosi alberghi e la passeggiata del lungolago. L'Axenstrasse, che si snoda lungo la sponda rocciosa del lago, porta in direzione di Altdorf e del San Gottardo.

What is generally known as the Lake of Lucerne also has a southeastern arm, the **Lake of Uri**. The resort of Brunnen with its lake promenade and numerous hotels can be seen in the left-hand foreground. The road running down the rocky shore is the famous Axenstrasse leading to Altdorf and the Gotthard.

Aus dem Nebelmeer, das über dem Wägital liegt, erhebt sich die schneebedeckte Flanke des **Turner** (2069 m ü. M.). An seinem Fusse beginnt eine reizvolle Wanderstrecke ins Klöntal und zum Pragelpass, der die Kantone Schwyz und Glarus verbindet.

Le flanc enneigé du **Turner** (2069 m) se détache de la mer de brouillard qui plane sur le Wägital. A ses pieds commence une charmante promenade vers le Klöntal et le col peu connu du Pragel qui réunit les cantons de Schwyz et de Glaris.

Dal mare di nebbia che ricopre la Wägital, si innalza il **Turner**, con i fianchi ricoperti di neve (2069 m.s.m.). Ai suoi piedi inizia una bellissima passeggiata che porta nella Klöntal, fino al Pragelpass, un passo poco conosciuto, che collega i cantoni di Svitto e Glarona.

The snow-clad flanks of the **Turner** (2069 metres) rise from the sea of cloud that fills the Wägital. From its foot there is an attractive hiking route into the Klöntal and to the little-known Pragel Pass which connects the cantons of Schwyz and Glarus.

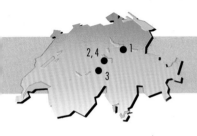

Svizzera centrale · Central Switzerland

1   2   3   4

Die ersten Strahlen der aufgehenden Sonne vergolden die Gipfel der **Fluebrig-Kette** (2093 m ü. M.) im Wägital (Kanton Schwyz). Das Tal mit dem gleichnamigen Stausee, nur 50 km von Zürich entfernt, ist ein beliebtes Ausflugsziel.

Stansstad am Vierwaldstättersee besass im Mittelalter als befestigter Hafenort eine strategisch wichtige Bedeutung. Die Autobahn Basel - Chiasso führt via Seelisberg- zum Gotthardtunnel.

Der **Lungernsee** und das Dorf Lungern (Kanton Obwalden) liegen an der Strecke zum Brünigpass (1008 m ü. M.), der die Innerschweiz mit dem Berner Oberland verbindet. Am linken oberen Bildrand ist das Pilatus-Massiv zu erkennen.

Blick vom **Stanserhorn** (1898 m ü. M.) auf Stansstad und den Vierwaldstättersee. Der See mit den sieben Becken verdankt seinen Namen den vier "Waldstätten" Uri, Schwyz, Unterwalden (Urkantone der Eidgenossenschaft) und Luzern.
Die Gegend um den Vierwaldstättersee zählt zu den traditionsreichsten Tourismusregionen der Schweiz.

Les premiers rayons du soleil levant dorent le sommet de la **chaîne de Fluebrig** (2093 m) au Wägital (canton de Schwyz). La vallée, avec son lac artificiel du même nom, à 50 km à peine de Zurich, est un but d'excursion apprécié.

Stansstad, au bord du lac des Quatre-Cantons, possédait au moyen âge, en tant que localité portuaire fortifiée, une importante position stratégique. L'autoroute Bâle-Chiasso conduit par le tunnel du Seelisberg au tunnel du Gothard.

Le **lac de Lungern** et le village de Lungern (canton d'Obwald) sont situés sur la route conduisant au col du Brünig (1008 m) qui relie la Suisse centrale à l'Oberland bernois. En haut à gauche, on reconnaît le massif du Pilate.

Perspective du **Stanserhorn** (1898 m) sur Stansstad et le lac des Quatre-Cantons. Le lac aux sept bassins doit son nom aux quatre "Waldstätten", Uri, Schwyz, Unterwald (cantons primitifs de la Confédération) et Lucerne.
La région autour du lac des Quatre-Cantons compte parmi les régions touristiques les plus traditionnelles du pays.

I primi raggi del sole che sorge indorano le vette della **catena del Fluebrig** (2093 m.s.m.), nella Wägital (Canton Svitto). La valle, con l'omonimo lago artificiale, a soli 50 km da Zurigo, è apprezzata meta di escursioni.

Nel Medioevo **Stansstad** era un porto fortificato di notevole importanza strategica. Attraverso la galleria del Seelisberg, l'autostrada Basilea - Chiasso porta verso la galleria del San Gottardo.

Il villaggio di **Lungern** (Canton Obwaldo), con il lago omonimo, è sulla strada che porta al passo del Brünig (1008 m.s.m.), che collega la Svizzera interna all'Oberland bernese. In alto a sinistra si riconosce il massiccio del Pilatus.

Uno sguardo dallo **Stanserhorn** (1898 m.s.m.) su Stansstad e il Lago dei Quattro Cantoni. Il lago, con i suoi sette bacini, deve il proprio nome ai quattro "Waldstätten" Uri, Svitto e Untervaldo (cantoni primitivi della Svizzera) e Lucerna.
La regione intorno al Lago dei Quattro Cantoni è una delle zone turistiche più ricche di tradizioni di tutta la Svizzera.

The first rays of the rising sun gild the summits of the **Fluebrig Chain** (2093 metres) in the Wägital, Canton of Schwyz. This valley with its storage lake, only 50 kilometres away from Zurich, is a popular goal for excursionists.

Stansstad on the Lake of Lucerne was a fortified port in the Middle Ages, when it was of considerable strategic importance. The Basle-Chiasso motorway today runs from here towards the Seelisberg Tunnel on its way to the Gotthard.

The village of Lungern in the Canton of Obwalden and its lake, the **Lungernsee**, lie on the road leading up to the Brünig Pass (1008 metres), which connects Central Switzerland with the Bernese Oberland. The massif of Mount Pilatus can be seen at top left.

Looking down from the **Stanserhorn** (1898 metres) on Stansstad and the Lake of Lucerne. The real name of this sheet of water is the Lake of the Four Forest Cantons, for its seven basins connect the three original Swiss cantons of Uri, Schwyz and Unterwalden, and Lucerne.
The lake and its surroundings form one of Switzerland's great traditional tourist regions.

1

2

3

Die Kantonshauptstadt **Zug** liegt am Ufer des gleichnamigen Sees. Von der spätgotischen Stadtanlage sind mehrere Türme und Teile der Stadtmauer erhalten. Heute ist Zug vor allem als Finanzplatz und "Steuerparadies" bekannt.

Zoug, chef-lieu cantonal, est situé sur la rive du lac du même nom. Plusieurs tours et parties des murs d'enceinte gothiques tardifs ont été conservés. Aujourd'hui, cette ville est surtout connue comme place financière et "paradis fiscal".

Zugo è la capitale dell'omonimo cantone e sorge sulle rive del lago, che pure porta lo stesso nome. Ancora oggi conserva parte delle mura e numerose torri delle fortificazioni che erano state erette a difesa della città. Oggigiorno Zugo è nota soprattutto come piazza finanziaria e "paradiso fiscale".

The town of **Zug** is capital of its canton, which, like the lake, shares its name. Several towers and parts of the walled defences have survived from the old Late Gothic town. Today Zug is well known for other reasons - as a financial centre and tax haven.

Ein treffenderer Name als **Fünffingerstöcke** hätte für die im Sustengebiet gelegene Gipfelgruppe kaum gewählt werden können. An der Passstrasse, die das Berner Oberland mit dem Urner Reusstal verbindet, liegt das Meiental mit dem Dörfchen Meien.

On n'aurait guère pu trouver de nom plus pertinent que "**Fünffingerstöcke**" (les monts des 5 doigts) à ce groupe de sommets situé dans la région de Susten. Le Meiental, avec le petit village de Meien, est situé sur la route du col qui relie l'Oberland bernois au Reusstal uranais.

Sarebbe stato difficile trovare un nome più adatto di **Fünffingerstöcke** (lett. picchi delle cinque dita) per il gruppo di montagne che sorgono nella regione del Susten. La strada del passo, che unisce l'Oberland bernese con il Canton Uri, si snoda lungo la Meiental, con il paesino di Meien.

This group of summits in the Susten region could hardly have been given a more fitting name than the **Fünffingerstöcke** - the "five-finger" massif. The Meien Valley with the hamlet of Meien lies on the pass road connecting the Bernese Oberland with Uri's Reuss Valley.

Am **Oberalp-Pass**: Blick auf Lutersee, Oberalpsee und Passhöhe (2044 m ü. M., links im Bild). Die 84 km lange Passstrasse verbindet das Urserental (Kanton Uri) mir dem Bündner Vorderrheintal.

Au **col d'Oberalp**: perspective sur le lac de Luter, le lac d'Oberalp et le sommet du col (2044 m, à gauche). La route du col longue de 84 km relie l'Urserental (canton d'Uri) à la vallée du Rhin antérieur dans les Grisons.

Sul **Passo dell'Oberalp**: una veduta dei due laghetti Lutersee e Oberalpsee e della regione del passo. La strada, della lunghezza di 84 km, unisce la Urserental (Canton Uri) con la valle del Reno anteriore, nel Canton Grigioni.

Looking down on the lakes of Lutersee and Oberalpsee and the top of the **Oberalp Pass** (2044 metres, top left). The pass road, 84 kilometres long, connects the Urseren Valley in the Canton of Uri with the Vorderrhein Valley in the Grisons.

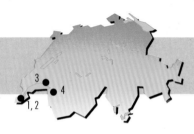

Région lémanique · Genfersee-Region

1

2

3

4

La ville de **Genève**, jadis cité du réformateur Calvin (1509 à 1564), est aujourd'hui surtout célèbre comme siège des organisations internationales (CICR, ONU, GATT). Mais en plus, la ville de l'extrémité occidentale du lac Léman est aussi une importante place financière et commerciale.

Die Stadt **Genf**, wo einst der Reformator Calvin (1509 bis 1564) wirkte, ist heute vor allem als Sitz internationaler Organisationen (IKRK, UNO, GATT) bekannt. Daneben ist die Stadt am westlichen Ende des Genfersees aber auch ein bedeutender Handels- und Finanzplatz.

La città di **Ginevra**, nella quale agì il riformatore Calvino (1509-1564), è nota oggigiorno soprattutto come sede di organizzazioni internazionali (CICR, ONU, GATT). Inoltre la città, che sorge all'estremità occidentale dell'omonimo lago, è una piazza commerciale e finanziaria di notevole interesse.

The city of **Geneva**, where the great reformer Calvin (1509-1564) was active, is today best known as the seat of international organizations (Red Cross, UN, GATT). But the city at the western end of its lake is also an important centre of trade and finance.

La nuit tombe sur Genève. Le **"Jet d'Eau"** est un symbole de la ville; avec une altitude de 130 mètres, il détient le record d'Europe.

Abendstimmung bei Genf. Der **"Jet d'Eau"** ist eines der Wahrzeichen der Stadt; die Fontäne schiesst 130 Meter in die Höhe und hält damit den Europa-Rekord.

Atmosfera serale a Ginevra. Il **"Jet d'Eau"** è uno dei simboli della città. La fontana lancia un getto alto 130 metri e detiene quindi il record europeo.

Sunset over Geneva and its **"Jet d'Eau"**. The fountain has become a landmark of the city. It rises to a height of 130 metres and is the highest anywhere in Europe.

La vue par-dessus l'extrémité orientale du **lac Léman** s'étend du delta de l'embouchure du Rhône au-dessus de la vallée du Rhône jusqu'aux paysages des vignobles valaisans. Le climat doux de la rive droite du lac a permis à la région de devenir une zone viticole réputée.
A gauche, la petite ville de Rivaz avec un château du 12ème siècle, surplombant la baie de Montreux, célèbre ville touristique et de congrès.

Der Blick über das östliche Ende des **Genfersees** reicht vom Flussdelta der Rhonemündung über das Rhonetal bis in die Walliser Gebirgswelt hinauf. Das milde Klima liess das Nordufer des Sees zu einem bekannten Weinanbaugebiet werden.
Links im Bild das Städtchen Rivaz mit einem Schloss aus dem 12. Jhdt., dahinter in der Bucht der bekannte Kur- und Kongressort Montreux.

Dall'estremità orientale del **Lago di Ginevra** si possono ammirare il delta e la valle del Rodano, lasciando spaziare lo sguardo fino alle montagne del Vallese. Il clima mite ha permesso alla riva destra del lago di diventare una zona vinicola molto apprezzata.
A sinistra nella foto si nota la cittadina di Rivaz, con un castello del 12. sec., più dietro, nell'insenatura, Montreux, famosa meta turistica e sede di innumerevoli congressi.

This shot of the eastern end of the **Lake of Geneva** extends from the delta at the mouth of the Rhone up the Rhone Valley to the mountains of the Valais. The mild climate has made the north shore of the lake a great wine-growing region.
On the left the little town of Rivaz with a castle from the 12th century, beyond it in the bay the well-known health resort and congress centre of Montreux.

Le **château** fort **d'Aigle** à un important point stratégique de la vallée du Rhône. Cette construction trapézoïdale avec trois tours circulaires et un "donjon" carré date du 12ème siècle. Le château abrite un musée du sel et du vin.

Das trutzige **Schloss Aigle** an strategisch wichtiger Lage im Rhonetal. Die trapezförmige Anlage mit drei Rundtürmen und einem viereckigen "Donjon" stammt aus dem 12. Jhdt. Das Schloss beherbergt ein Wein- und Salzmuseum.

Il possente **Castello di Aigle**, in posizione strategica nella valle del Rodano. La fortificazione, a base trapezoidale con tre torri rotonde e un torrione a base quadrata, risale al 12. sec. Il castello ospita un museo del vino e del sale.

The defiant-looking **Aigle Castle** lies in a strategically important position in the Rhone Valley. The castle with its trapezoidal layout, its three round towers and rectangular keep was built in the 12th century. Today it houses a wine and salt museum.

1

2

3

Le **château** savoyard **de Chillon**, au bord du lac Léman, fait partie des fort médiévaux les plus célèbres de Suisse. Le rocher sur la rive du lac, sur lequel le château a été érigé au 13ème siècle, est fortifié depuis le 9ème siècle.

Lausanne, la capitale du canton de Vaud, est dominée par la cathédrale Notre-Dame, incontestablement la plus belle construction gothique de Suisse. Cette église, aujourd'hui réformée, est mentionnée pour la première fois en 814 comme basilique carolingienne. Avant et après la Réforme, la cathédrale a été plusieurs fois transformée et agrandie.
Lausanne abrite différents musées d'art importants.

La **Vallée de Joux** est située dans le Jura vaudois, non loin de la frontière française. Dans cette vallée d'altitude située à plus de 1000 m, les hivers peuvent être très rigoureux; le lac de Joux est ainsi généralement gelé. La perspective plonge de l'extrémité du lac direction sud-ouest; à gauche, le village L'Abbaye.

Das savoyische **Schloss Chillon** am Genfersee zählt zu den bekanntesten mittelalterlichen Burgen der Schweiz. Der Felsen am Seeufer, auf dem das Schloss im 13. Jhdt. erbaut wurde, ist seit dem 9. Jhdt. befestigt.

Lausanne, die Hauptstadt des Kantons Waadt, wird von der Kathedrale Notre-Dame überragt, dem unbestritten schönsten gotischen Bauwerk der Schweiz. Die heute reformierte Kirche wurde erstmals im Jahre 814 als karolingische Basilika erwähnt. Vor und nach der Reformation wurde die Kathedrale mehrfach umgebaut und erweitert.
Lausanne beherbergt verschiedene bedeutende Kunstmuseen.

Im Waadtländer Jura, unweit der französischen Grenze, liegt das **Vallée de Joux**. In diesem über 1000 m ü. M. gelegenen Hochtal kann es im Winter empfindlich kalt werden; der Lac de Joux ist denn auch meistens zugefroren. Der Blick geht vom Ende des Sees in südwestliche Richtung; links im Bild das Dorf L'Abbaye.

Il **castello** sabaudo **di Chillon** sul Lago di Ginevra, è uno delle roccaforti medievali più famose della Svizzera. Lo scoglio sulla riva del lago, sul quale venne costruito il castello nel 13. sec., era già stato fortificato nel 9. sec.

Nell'immagine di **Losanna**, capitale del Canton Vaud, domina la cattedrale di Notre-Dame, indubbiamente la costruzione gotica più bella della Svizzera. La chiesa, oggigiorno di culto protestante, viene menzionata per la prima volta nell'anno 814, come basilica carolinga. La cattedrale è stata oggetto di numerosi ampliamenti e trasformazioni, prima e dopo il periodo della Riforma.
Losanna ospita numerosi musei artistici di notevole importanza.

Nel Giura vodese, a poca distanza dal confine francese, si estende la **Vallée de Joux**. In questa alta valle, situata ad oltre 1000 m.s.m., gli inverni possono essere particolarmente rigidi e generalmente fanno gelare anche il Lac de Joux. Il panorama si estende dall'estremità del lago in direzione sud-ovest; a sinistra nella foto il villaggio di L'Abbaye.

The Savoyard **Château de Chillon** on the Lake of Geneva is one of Switzerland's most famous medieval castles. The rocks on the lake shore on which the castle was built in the 13th century had been fortified as early as the 9th century.

The capital of the Canton of Vaud, **Lausanne** is overtopped by the Cathedral of Notre-Dame, by common consent Switzerland's finest Gothic building. A Carolingian basilica on this site is first mentioned in 814. The cathedral, now Protestant, was altered and extended on several occasions before and after the Reformation. Lausanne also boasts several prestigious art museums.

Not far from the French frontier, in the part of the Jura belonging to the Canton of Vaud, lies the **Vallée de Joux**. It can be very cold in this valley at an altitude of over 1000 metres, and the waters of the Lac de Joux mostly freeze over in winter. We are here looking southwest from the end of the lake, with the village of L'Abbaye on the left.

Fribourg · Freiburg · Friborgo · Neuchâtel · Neuenburg

1

2

3

4

5

Au bord de la vieille ville de **Fribourg** (Freiburg), la capitale bilingue du canton du même nom. De nombreuses tours et parties des anciennes fortifications le long des rives de la Sarine datant du 15ème siècle ont été bien conservées.

Am Rand der Innenstadt von **Freiburg** (Fribourg), der zweisprachigen Hauptstadt des gleichnamigen Kantons. Von den Befestigungsanlagen entlang des Saaneufers sind zahlreiche Türme und Mauerstücke aus dem 15. Jhdt. gut erhalten.

La cerchia esterna di **Friburgo**, la capitale bilingue dell'omonimo cantone. Delle fortificazioni lungo le rive della Sarine si sono conservate fino ai nostri giorni numerose torri e tratti di mura risalenti al 15. sec.

A scene on the edge of the town of **Fribourg** (Freiburg), the bilingual capital of the canton of the same name. Many of the fifteenth-century towers and walls of the former fortifications along the River Sarine are still in a good state of repair.

Gruyères, canton de Fribourg, connue également par son fromage du même nom, a su préserver jusqu'à nos jours son aspect médiéval avec des ouvrages de fortification et murs d'enceinte. Le château, situé sur le point le plus haut de cette petite ville construite sur une colline, date du 12ème siècle.

Gruyères im Kanton Freiburg, auch bekannt durch den gleichnamigen Käse, konnte bis heute sein mittelalterliches Aussehen mit Befestigungswerken und Stadtmauer erhalten. Das Schloss, auf dem höchsten Punkt des auf einem Hügel erbauten Städtchens gelegen, stammt aus dem 12. Jhdt.

Gruyères nel Canton Friburgo, nota anche per l'omonimo formaggio, è riuscita a conservare fino ad oggi il suo aspetto medievale, con le opere di fortificazione e le mura cittadine. Il castello, che si erge nel punto più alto della collina sui cui sorge la graziosa cittadina, risale al 12. sec.

The town of **Gruyères** in the Canton of Fribourg has given its name to a well-known cheese. It has preserved its medieval aspect with fortifications and town walls. The castle, perched on the highest point of the hill-top town, dates from the 12th century.

C'est à **Font**, au bord du lac de Neuchâtel, que se trouvent trois constructions historiques: l'église de St. Sulpice dont la nef a été construite vers 1560, le château du 16ème siècle, ancien siège des baillis, et les fortifications construites vers l'an 1000 dont il ne reste que des vestiges.

In **Font** am Neuenburger See befinden sich drei historische Bauten: Die Kirche St. Sulpice, deren Schiff um 1560 erbaut wurde, das Schloss aus dem 16. Jhdt., ehemaliger Sitz von Landvögten, und die um das Jahr 1000 erbaute Festungsanlage, von der nur Mauerreste übrigblieben.

Font, sul Lago di Neuchâtel, può vantare tre costruzioni storiche: la chiesa di St. Sulpice, la cui navata risale al 1560, il castello del 16. sec., già sede dei balivi, e le fortificazioni, costruite intorno all'anno 1000, delle quali sono rimasti solo alcuni tratti delle mura.

There are three historic buildings at **Font** on the Lake of Neuchâtel: the church of St. Sulpice, with a nave built around 1560; the 16th-century castle, and the fortifications dating from about 1000, of which only parts of the walls have survived.

Neuchâtel, chef-lieu cantonal situé au bord du lac du même nom, est dominé par deux constructions qui méritent d'être relevées: le château et la collégiale de Notre-Dame avec sa basilique à trois nefs.

Die Kantonshauptstadt **Neuenburg**, am gleichnamigen See gelegen, wird von zwei bemerkenswerten Bauwerken dominiert: Dem Schloss und der Kollegiatskirche Notre-Dame mit der Stiftskirche in Form einer dreischiffigen Basilika.

Su **Neuchâtel**, la capitale cantonale che sorge sull'omonimo lago, dominano due costruzioni di notevole importanza: il castello e la collegiata di Notre-Dame, con la chiesa in forma di basilica a tre navate.

The town of **Neuchâtel** has given its name both to the lake on which it stands and to the canton of which it is the capital. It is dominated by two impressive buildings: the castle, and the collegiate church of Notre-Dame in the form of a three-aisled basilica.

Auvernier, au bord du lac de Neuchâtel, a un passé historique très ancien (vestiges préhistoriques). L'église réformée (à gauche) date du 15ème siècle; le château a été construit au 16ème siècle.

Auvernier am Neuenburgersee hat eine geschichtliche Vergangenheit, die weit zurückreicht (prähistorische Fundstätte). Aus dem 15. Jhdt. stammt die reformierte Kirche (links im Bild); die Schlossanlage wurde im 16. Jhdt. erbaut.

Auvernier, sul lago di Neuchâtel, ha un passato che risale alla notte dei tempi (gli scavi hanno fornito interessanti reperti preistorici). La chiesa protestante risale al 15. sec. (a sinistra nella foto); il castello fortificato venne costruito nel 16. sec.

Auvernier on the Lake of Neuchâtel is a village with a long past, for excavations here have yielded prehistoric finds. The Protestant church (left) goes back to the 15th century, the castle was built in the 16th.

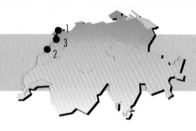

1

2

3

La petite ville de **Porrentruy**, canton du Jura. Au centre, l'hôtel de ville, derrière lui, l'église St. Pierre, une basilique gothique du 14ème siècle.
L'activisme autonomiste des Jurassiens a été récompensé en 1978 par la création de leur canton.

Le **lac des Brenets** est situé dans la vallée du Doubs. Le Doubs forme dans le Jura sur de longues distances la frontière franco-suisse; ici, la section de la frontière commence aux Brenets.

La **Bosse** vers Saignelégier (canton du Jura). Ce haut-plateau des Franches-Montagnes est célèbre pour l'élevage de chevaux; des pâturages délicatement vallonnés caractérisent le paysage. Le Marché Concours annuel de Saignelégier, avec des concours hippiques, est une grande attraction de la région.

Das Städtchen **Pruntrut** im Kanton Jura. In der Bildmitte das "Hôtel de Ville", dahinter die Kirche St. Pierre, eine gotische Basilika aus dem 14. Jhdt.
Die Autonomiebestrebungen der Jurassier wurden im Jahre 1978 mit der Kantonsgründung belohnt.

Im Tal des Doubs liegt der **Lac des Brenets**. Der Doubs bildet im Jura über weite Strecken die schweizerisch-französische Grenze; hier bei Les Brenets beginnt dieser Grenzabschnitt.

La **Bosse** bei Saignelégier (Kanton Jura). Das Hochplateau der Freiberge ist bekannt als Pferdezuchtgebiet; sanfte Weiden prägen die Landschaft. Eine besondere Attraktion ist der "Marché Concours" von Saignelégier mit pferdesportlichen Wettbewerben.

La cittadina di **Porrentruy** nel canton Giura. Al centro della foto l'"Hôtel de Ville", dietro la chiesa di St. Pierre, una basilica gotica del 14. sec.
Le tendenze autonomistiche dei giurassiani sono state premiate nel 1978 con la costituzione del loro cantone.

Nella valle del Doubs si trova il **Lac des Brenets**. Nel Giura il Doubs segna su lunghi tratti il confine franco-svizzero; qui, in corrispondenza di Les Brenets, inizia un tratto di confine.

La **Bosse** a Saignelégier (Canton Giura). L'altipiano delle Franches Montagnes è molto rinomato per l'allevamento dei cavalli; il paesaggio è caratterizzato dai pascoli ondulati. Una particolare attrazione è costituita dal "Marché Concours" di Saignelégier, che comprende numerose gare ippiche.

The little town of **Porrentruy** in the Canton of the Jura. At the centre the Hôtel de Ville or Town Hall, behind it the church of Saint-Pierre, a Gothic basilica from the 14th century.
The people of the Jura won their struggle for autonomy in 1978, when the Canton of Jura was created.

The River Doubs widens at one point in its course to form a lake, the **Lac des Brenets**. From this point northwards the river marks the Franco-Swiss frontier in the Jura.

La **Bosse** near Saignelégier in the Jura. The high plateau of the Franches Montagnes is a well-known horse-breeding region. Gently rolling pastures characterize the landscape. The annual "Marché Concours" in Saignelégier, a market with equestrian events, attracts horse-lovers from far and wide.

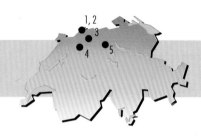

Nordwestschweiz · Nord-ouest de la Suisse

1

2

3

4

5

Wahrzeichen der Industriestadt **Basel** ist das Münster aus dem 12. bis 15. Jhdt. Davor die Pfalz, eine baumbestandene Aussichtsterrasse über dem Rhein, der die Schweiz beim Dreiländereck (D/F/CH) in Richtung Nordsee verlässt.

La cathédrale, bâtie du 12ème au 15ème siècle, est le symbole de **Bâle**, ville industrielle. Devant celle-ci, la Pfalz, une terrasse panoramique arborée au-dessus du Rhin qui quitte la Suisse à l'intersection des trois frontières (RFA/F/CH) à destination de la mer du Nord.

Simbolo della città industriale di **Basilea** è la cattedrale, eretta fra il 12. e il 15. sec. Davanti si nota la Pfalz, una terrazza panoramica alberata sul Reno, il quale esce dalla Svizzera in corrispondenza del cosiddetto Dreiländereck (l'angolo delle tre nazioni), in direzione del Mare del Nord.

The minster, built from the 12th to the 15th century, is the chief landmark of the city of **Basle**. In front of it is a tree-shaded terrace above the River Rhine, which leaves Switzerland for the North Sea at the Dreiländereck close by, the place where the French, German and Swiss frontiers meet.

Der Rhein stellt die einzige schiffbare Verbindung der Schweiz mit den Weltmeeren dar. In den Anlagen des **Basler Rheinhafens**, die mit Rundfahrtschiffen besichtigt werden können, werden vor allem Massengüter umgeladen.

Le Rhin représente l'unique voie de communication navigable de la Suisse avec les mers du monde. Les **installations portuaires de Bâle**, qui peuvent être visitées en bateau avec des circuits organisés, servent surtout au transbordement des marchandises de gros tonnage.

Per la Svizzera il Reno rappresenta l'unico collegamento navigabile con i mari del mondo. Gli impianti del **porto fluviale di Basilea**, che si possono visitare con i battelli turistici, servono soprattutto per il trasbordo di merci di massa.

The Rhine is Switzerland's only navigable outlet to the ocean. The **Rhine Port at Basle**, which can be toured by special boat services, is chiefly engaged in loading and unloading bulk goods.

Wenn in tieferen Lagen der Nebel liegenbleibt, scheint auf dem **Belchen** (1100 m ü. M.) im Kanton Baselland die Sonne. Der Hügelzug zwischen Sissach und Olten gehört zum Juramassiv.

Quand les vallées sont enfouies sous le brouillard, le soleil brille sur le **Belchen** (1100 m), canton de Bâle-Campagne. Cette chaîne de collines entre Sissach et Olten fait partie du massif du Jura.

Quando la pianura resta sotto una coltre di nebbia, sul **Belchen** (1100 m.s.m.), nel Cantone Basilea-Campagna, splende il sole. La catena di colline che si estende da Sissach a Olten fa parte del massiccio del Giura.

When mist lies in the valleys, the sun is often shining on the **Belchen** (1100 metres) in the Canton of Basle-Campagne. This range of hills between Sissach and Olten forms part of the Jura massif.

Die Kantonshauptstadt **Solothurn** weist eine geschlossene Altstadt auf, wie sie nur noch selten zu sehen ist. Überragt wird der alte Stadtteil von der ersten klassizistischen Kirche der Schweiz, der Kathedrale St. Ursen, die 1773 fertiggestellt wurde.

Soleure, chef-lieu cantonal, présente une vieille ville d'une rare homogénéité. La partie ancienne de la ville est dominée par l'une des premières églises néo-classiques de Suisse, la cathédrale de St. Ursen, achevée en 1773.

A **Soletta**, capitale cantonale, la città vecchia è veramente omogenea, cosa ormai piuttosto rara a vedersi. Sulla città sovrasta la prima chiesa classicistica della Svizzera, la cattedrale di St. Ursen, terminata nel 1773.

The cantonal capital of **Solothurn** has an Old Town of rare compactness lying at the foot of Switzerland's first Neo-Classical church, the cathedral of St. Ursus, which was completed in 1773.

Das landschaftlich reizvolle Seetal zwischen Lenzburg (Kanton Aargau) und Luzern verdankt seinen Namen zwei Seen: dem Baldeggersee und dem **Hallwilersee** (im Bild), der unter Naturschutz steht.

Les charmants paysages du Seetal s'étendent entre Lenzburg (canton d'Argovie) et Lucerne et doivent leur nom à deux lacs: le lac de Baldegger et le **lac de Hallwil** (sur la photo) qui est une zone protégée.

La graziosa regione della Seetal, fra Lenzburg (Canton Argovia) e Lucerna, deve il suo nome a due laghi: il Baldeggersee e l'**Hallwilersee** (in figura), che è una zona protetta.

The Seetal, or Lake Valley, running from Lenzburg in the Canton of Aargau to Lucerne, is a landscape of great charm. It owes its name to its two lakes, the Baldeggersee and the **Hallwilersee** (shown here), which is under nature conservancy.

1

2

Schon in der Römerzeit wurden die Thermalquellen und die strategisch günstige Lage dieses Ortes an der Limmat geschätzt. Daraus entwickelte sich die heutige Kur- und Bäderstadt **Baden** (Kanton Aargau), die auch Sitz bedeutender Industriebetriebe ist.

A l'époque romaine, on appréciait déjà les sources thermales et la situation stratégiquement favorable de cette localité des bords de la Limmat. C'est ainsi que s'est développée la ville touristique et thermale actuelle de **Baden** (canton d'Argovie), siège de nombreuses entreprises industrielles.

Già ai tempi dei Romani venivano apprezzate sia le fonti termali che la posizione strategica di questa località in riva alla Limmat. Con il trascorrere dei secoli si sviluppò poi la città di **Baden** (Canton Argovia), rinomata come stazione climatica e per i suoi bagni termali. Inoltre è sede di importanti stabilimenti industriali.

The strategic situation of this town and its hot springs were already appreciated by the Romans. Today **Baden** on the River Limmat in the Canton of Aargau is a well-known watering-place (its name means "baths") as well as possessing extensive industries.

Rudolf von Habsburg erteilte **Bremgarten** im Jahre 1256 das Stadtrecht. Die mittelalterliche und barocke Bausubstanz konnte bis heute erhalten werden. Eine gedeckte Holzbrücke über die Reuss aus dem Jahre 1544 verbindet die Oberstadt mit der Unterstadt. In der Bildmitte das Schlössli (1641) und der zur Stadtbefestigung zählende Spittelturm.

Rodolphe de Habsbourg accorda à **Bremgarten** en 1256 les droits de cité. La substance architecturale médiévale et baroque a pu être conservée jusqu'à nos jours. Un pont couvert en bois au-dessus de la Reuss datant de 1544 relie la ville supérieure aux quartiers inférieurs. Au centre, le petit château (1641) et le Spittelturm qui faisait partie des fortifications de la ville.

Rodolfo d'Absburgo elevò **Bremgarten** al rango di città nel 1256. Gli edifici medievali e barocchi hanno potuto essere conservati fino ad oggi. Un ponte coperto che attraversa la Reuss, costruito nel 1544, unisce la frazione della città alta con quella bassa. Al centro dell'illustrazione si nota il piccolo castello e la Spittelturm, che faceva parte delle fortificazioni della città.

Rudolf of Habsburg granted **Bremgarten** its charter in 1256. Many of its medieval and Baroque buildings have survived till the present day. A covered wooden bridge over the Reuss, dating from 1544, connects the upper and lower parts of the town. At the centre of our picture the small castle (1641) and the Spittel Tower, which was part of the old town defences.

65

Zürich · Zurich · Zurigo

1

2

3

4

Blick über **Zürich**, die "heimliche Hauptstadt" der Schweiz. In der Bildmitte Limmatquai und Grossmünster; rechts Fraumünster und Kirche St. Peter. Im Vordergrund rechts das Schweizerische Landesmuseum und die als "Needle Park" zu trauriger Berühmtheit gelangte Parkanlage "Platzspitz".

Die geschlossene Häusergruppe **"Zur Schipfe"**, im 17. und 18. Jhdt. in der heute noch erhaltenen Form erbaut, liegt am östlichen Fuss eines Moränenhügels des eiszeitlichen Linthgletschers. Hier, auf dem Lindenhof, bauten die Römer im 4. Jhdt. ein Kastell.
Limmat- und Seefahrten auf Kursschiffen gehören zu den beliebtesten Touristenattraktionen Zürichs.

Seit seiner Gründung im 13. Jhdt. hat sich das auf einem Jura-Ausläufer gelegene Städtchen **Regensberg** seinen mittelalterlichen Charakter erhalten können. Das Schloss mit markantem Rundturm ist von weither zu erkennen.

Auf einer Halbinsel im Rhein, inmitten sonniger Rebhänge, liegt die ehemalige Benediktinerabtei **Rheinau**. Die im Jahre 844 erstmals erwähnte Abtei besteht heute aus einem grossen Klosterkomplex mit Stiftskirche in spätgotisch-barockem Stil.

Vue embrassant **Zurich**, la "capitale secrète" de la Suisse. Au centre, le Limmatquai et le Grossmünster, à droite le Fraumünster et l'église St. Peter. Au premier plan à droite, le Musée national suisse et le "Platzspitz", tristement célèbre comme "Needle Park".

Le groupe homogène de maisons **"Zur Schipfe"**, construit aux 17ème et 18ème siècles dans la forme encore préservée actuellement, se situe au pied oriental de la colline morainique du glacier de la Linth de l'ère glaciaire. Ici, au Lindenhof, les Romains avaient construit un fort au 4ème siècle.
Des croisières en bateau sur la Limmat et le lac font partie des attractions touristiques les plus appréciées de Zurich.

Depuis sa fondation au 13ème siècle, la petite ville de **Regensberg**, située sur un contrefort du Jura, a pu conserver son caractère médiéval. Le château, dominé par sa tour circulaire, est reconnaissable de loin.

L'ancienne abbaye bénédictine, **Rheinau**, est située sur une presqu'île sur le Rhin, au coeur de vignobles ensoleillés. Cette abbaye, mentionnée pour la première fois en 844, est aujourd'hui composée d'un grand complexe monastique avec basilique, de style baroque-gothique tardif.

Veduta di **Zurigo**, la "capitale segreta" della Svizzera. Al centro il Limmatquai e il Grossmünster, a destra le chiese di Fraumünster e St. Peter. A destra, il Museo nazionale svizzero e il tristemente famoso "Platzspitz", trasformato in "Needle Park".

Il gruppo compatto di case **"Zur Schipfe"**, costruite nel 17. e 18. sec. e conservate fino ad oggi nella loro forma originaria, si erge ai piedi di una collina morenica lasciata nell'era glaciale dal ghiacciaio della Linth. Qui, sul Lindenhof, nel 4. sec. i Romani costruirono un castello.
Le escursioni sulla Limmat e sul lago con battelli di linea sono fra le più frequentate attrazioni turistiche di Zurigo.

Dalla sua fondazione nel 13. sec., la cittadina di **Regensberg**, situata sulle propaggini del Giura, ha saputo conservare il suo carattere medievale. Il castello, con il suo imponente torrione rotondo, si riconosce da lontano.

Su una penisola nel Reno, in mezzo ai pendii di soleggiati vigneti, si erge quella che una volta era l'abbazia benedettina di **Rheinau**. Oggigiorno l'abbazia è un grande convento, con collegiata in stile tardo-gotico-barocco.

Zurich is sometimes referred to as the "secret capital of Switzerland". At the centre the Limmatquai and Grossmünster; on the right Fraumünster and St. Peter's. In the right-hand foreground the Swiss National Museum and the Platzspitz, now known as "Needle Park" because of the junkies who frequent it.

The compact group of houses known as the **"Schipfe"** has been preserved as it was built in the 17th and 18th centuries. It lies at the eastern foot of a moraine formed by the Linth Glacier in the last Ice Age. The Romans built a citadel on top of this hill in the 4th century, on what is now the Lindenhof.
Boat services on the River Limmat and the lake are among Zurich's most popular tourist attractions.

The little town of **Regensberg**, situated on a marginal ridge of the Jura, has preserved its medieval appearance since its founding in the 13th century. The castle with its conspicuous round tower can be seen from far around.

The former Benedictine abbey of **Rheinau** lies among sunny vineyards on a peninsula in the Rhine. The abbey is first mentioned in 844. Today the buildings form a large monastery complex with a collegiate church in Late Gothic and Baroque styles.

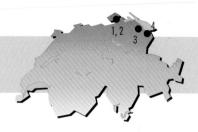

1

2

3

4

Die Kantonshauptstadt Schaffhausen wird überragt vom Schloss **Munot** (erbaut 1564 bis 85), einem in dieser Grösse einmaligen Befestigungswerk. Die Altstadt am Rheinufer ist seit dem 14. Jhdt. praktisch unverändert erhalten geblieben.

Schaffhouse, chef-lieu cantonal, est surplombé par le château de **Munot** (construit entre 1564 et 1585), un ouvrage de fortification unique par ses dimensions. La vieille ville sur les rives du Rhin est restée pratiquement inchangée depuis le 14ème siècle.

Su Sciaffusa, capitale cantonale, sovrasta il castello di **Munot** (costruito fra il 1564 e il 1585), una fortificazione eccezionale per le sue dimensioni. La città vecchia, sulle rive del Reno, è rimasta praticamente immutata dal 14. sec.

Above the cantonal capital of Schaffhausen towers the **Munot**, a fortress built in 1564 to 1585 and unequalled in size in Switzerland. The Old Town on the banks of the Rhine has remained practically unchanged since the 14th century.

Der **Rheinfall**, einer der grössten Wasserfälle Europas, zählt zu den berühmtesten Naturschauspielen der Schweiz. Beim Schloss Laufen (rechts im Bild), wenig unterhalb der Stadt Schaffhausen, stürzen pro Sekunde durchschnittlich 1000 Kubikmeter Wasser über eine 175 m breite und 23 m hohe Felsstufe stiebend in die Tiefe. Der Felsen in der Mitte kann per Schiff erreicht und zu Fuss bestiegen werden.

Les **chutes du Rhin**, l'une des plus grandes chutes d'eau d'Europe, s'inscrivent parmi les plus célèbres curiosités naturelles de Suisse. Vers le château de Laufen (à droite sur la photo), un peu en-dessous de la ville de Schaffhouse, ce ne sont pas moins de 1000 m3 d'eau en moyenne qui dévalent par seconde sur une largeur de 175 m une dénivellation rocheuse de 23 m. Le rocher au centre peut être atteint en bateau et escaladé à pied.

Le **Cascate del Reno** sono fra le cascate più grandi d'Europa e sicuramente uno degli spettacoli naturali più belli della Svizzera. In corrispondenza del castello di Laufen (a destra nella foto) precipitano fra enormi spruzzi in media 1000 metri cubi al secondo, cadendo da un gradino di roccia largo 175 m e alto 23 m. Allo scoglio che si trova al centro del fiume si può arrivare con un battellino. Una ripida scala permette di salire fino alla sua sommità.

The **Rhine Falls**, one of Europe's largest waterfalls, is also one of Switzerland's most impressive natural spectacles. Near Laufen Castle (top right), not far from Schaffhausen, some 1000 cubic metres of water plunge down each second in a mist of spray over a rock barrier 175 metres across and 23 metres high. The rock in the middle can be reached by boat and climbed for a better view.

Schloss Hagenwil, eine prachtvolle Wasserburg mit Zugbrücke in der Nähe des thurgauischen Städtchens Amriswil, wurde im 13. Jhdt. erbaut. In der als Wehrgang ausgelegten Galerie befindet sich seit über 150 Jahren eine Gastwirtschaft.

Le **château de Hagenwil**, un somptueux château fort entouré d'eau avec pont-levis à proximité de la petite ville thurgovienne d'Amriswil, a été construit au 13ème siècle. La galerie, initialement le chemin de ronde, abrite depuis plus de 150 ans une auberge.

Il **castello di Hagenwil** è una magnifica roccaforte, con tanto di acqua e ponte levatoio, situata nelle vicinanze della cittadina turgoviese di Amriswil. La costruzione risale al 13. sec. Nella galleria, dove originariamente passava la ronda, è in funzione da oltre 150 anni un ristorante tipico.

Hagenwil Castle, a splendid water-girt fortress with a drawbridge situated near the town of Amriswil in Thurgau, was built in the 13th century. For the last 150 years or more a restaurant has been accommodated in the gallery, originally designed as battlements.

Abendstimmung bei Rorschach am **Bodensee**, der zwischen Altenrhein und Stein am Rhein die schweizerisch-deutsche Grenze bildet. Im Umkreis des Bodensees konnten zahlreiche steinzeitliche Siedlungsspuren nachgewiesen werden.

La nuit tombe sur Rorschach, au bord du **lac de Constance**, formant la frontière germano-suisse entre Altenrhein et Stein am Rhein. Dans la région du lac de Constance, on a pu trouver de nombreuses traces de colonies datant de l'âge de la pierre.

Atmosfera serale sul **Lago di Costanza**, che fra Altenrhein e Stein am Rhein marca il confine fra la Svizzera e la Germania. Intorno al Lago di Costanza è stato possibile trovare le tracce di numerosi villaggi dell'età della pietra.

Evening light over Rorschach on the **Lake of Constance**, which forms the Swiss frontier with Germany between Altenrhein and Stein am Rhein. Traces of Stone Age settlements have been found at many places around the Lake of Constance.

Ostschweiz · Suisse orientale

1

2

3

4

5

Die Kantonshauptstadt **St. Gallen** liegt zwischen Bodensee und Alpstein-Massiv. Links im Bild die Kathedrale, ein eindrucksvolles Beispiel barocker Baukunst. Ihre Stiftsbibliothek enthält eine reiche Sammlung mittelalterlicher Handschriften.

Das **Appenzellerland** ist reich an landschaftlich reizvollen Gegenden. Der 2502 m hohe Säntis (im Hintergrund), die höchste Erhebung des Alpstein-Massivs, ist mit einer Luftseilbahn von der Schwägalp aus bequem erreichbar.

Vom Luftkurort **Heiden** aus bietet sich ein herrlicher Panoramablick auf den Bodensee, der mit dem Auto über eine kurvenreiche Strasse oder mit einer Zahnradbahn erreicht wird. Ein Denkmal im Ort erinnert daran, dass Henri Dunant hier seine letzten Lebensjahre verbrachte.

Der Dorfplatz von **Gais**, Kanton Appenzell Ausserrhoden. Die traditionellen Holz- und Steinhäuser mit ihren charakteristisch geschweiften Giebeln entstanden nach einer Feuersbrunst im Jahre 1780.

Als "kleinste historische Stadt der Schweiz" wird **Werdenberg** im St. Galler Rheintal bezeichnet. Sehenswert sind die hervorragend erhaltenen Holzhäuser und das Schloss der einstmaligen Grafen von Werdenberg aus dem 12. bis 17. Jhdt.

St. Gall, chef-lieu cantonal, est situé entre le lac de Constance et le massif d'Alpstein. A gauche de l'illustration, la cathédrale, un exemple impressionnant de l'art baroque. La bibliothèque de son évêché abrite une riche collection de manuscrits médiévaux.

Le **pays d'Appenzell** est riche en régions aux paysages pittoresques. Le Säntis (arrière-plan), culminant à 2502 m, est la plus haute élévation du massif d'Alpstein et peut être confortablement atteint en téléphérique depuis la Schwägalp.

A partir de la station climatique de **Heiden**, on profite d'un panorama somptueux sur le lac de Constance qui peut être atteint en voiture par une route très sinueuse ou en chemin de fer à crémaillère. Un monument rappelle qu'Henri Dunant a passé ici les dernières années de sa vie.

La place du village de **Gais**, canton d'Appenzell Rhodes-Extérieures. Les traditonnelles maisons en bois et pierre, avec leurs pignons arqués caractéristiques, ont été construites en 1780 après un incendie.

On dit de **Werdenberg**, dans la vallée du Rhin saint-galloise, qu'elle est la "plus petite cité historique de Suisse". Les maisons en bois magnifiquement conservées et le château où vivait autrefois le comte de Werdenberg, contruits entre le 12ème et le 17ème siècle, méritent un détour.

San Gallo, capitale dell'omonimo cantone, è situata fra il Lago di Costanza e il massiccio dell'Alpstein. A sinistra la cattedrale, un interessante esempio di architettura barocca. La sua biblioteca comprende una ricca collezione di manoscritti medievali.

L'**Appenzello** è una regione ricca di posti graziosissimi. Il Säntis, alto 2502 m (sullo sfondo), la cima più alta del massiccio dell'Alpstein, può essere comodamente raggiunto con una funivia che parte dalla Schwägalp.

Dalla stazione climatica di **Heiden** si può godere un magnifico panorama sul Lago di Costanza. Vi si arriva lungo una strada ricca di curve o con il treno a cremagliera. Un monumento ricorda che Henri Dunant vi passò gli ultimi anni della sua vita.

La piazza del paese di **Gais**, nel Cantone di Appenzello esterno. Le tradizionali case di legno e pietra, con i caratteristici tetti curvi, vennero costruite dopo un grave incendio, scoppiato nel 1780.

Werdenberg, nella valle del Reno, vicino a San Gallo, viene detta la "più piccola città storica della Svizzera". Degne di essere viste sono soprattutto le case di legno, magnificamente conservate, e il castello, una costruzione che va dal 12. al 17. sec.

Capital of the canton of the same name, **St. Gallen** lies between the Lake of Constance and the Alpstein massif. On the left the cathedral, an imposing example of Baroque architecture. Its collegiate library owns a rich collection of medieval manuscripts.

The two half-cantons of **Appenzell** have some beautiful scenery to offer. The Säntis in the background, at 2502 metres the highest summit of the Alpstein massif, can be reached by aerial cableway from Schwägalp.

There is a wonderful view from the health resort of **Heiden** of the Lake of Constance, which can be reached either by car down a winding road or else by rack railway. A monument in the village recalls the fact that Henri Dunant, founder of the Red Cross, spent his last years here.

Village square in **Gais**, Canton of Appenzell Ausserrhoden. These traditional houses of wood or stone with their characteristic curved gables were built after a big fire in 1780.

Werdenberg in the Rhine Valley in the Canton of St. Gallen is sometimes called the "smallest historic town in Switzerland". The very well preserved wooden houses and the castle of the former Count of Werdenberg, dating from the 12th to 17th centuries, more than repay a visit.

1

2

3

Die Hafenstadt **Rapperswil** (Kanton St. Gallen) mit interessanten historischen Gebäuden liegt am oberen Ende des Zürichsees. Das Schloss, eine mächtige Dreiecksanlage aus dem späten 12. Jhdt., überragt die Altstadt.

La ville portuaire de **Rapperswil** (canton de St. Gall), avec des intéressantes constructions historiques, est située à l'extrémité supérieure du lac de Zurich. Le château, une impressionnante construction triangulaire de la fin du 12ème siècle, surplombe la vieille ville.

La città di **Rapperswil** (Canton San Gallo), con il porto e interessanti edifici storici, si trova all'estremità superiore del Lago di Zurigo. Il castello, un'imponente roccaforte del tardo 12. sec., sovrasta la città.

The port of **Rapperswil** lies at the upper end of the Lake of Zurich in the Canton of St. Gallen and boasts some interesting historic buildings. The castle, a massy fortress with a triangular layout from the late 12th century, looks down on the old quarter of the town.

Blick auf **Weesen** am westlichen Ende des Walensees (Kanton St. Gallen). Als der Warentransport zwischen Zürich und Graubünden streckenweise noch per Schiff abgewickelt wurde, war Weesen ein wichtiger Hafenort.

Vue sur **Weesen**, à l'extrémité occidentale du Walensee (canton de St. Gall). Lorsque le transport des marchandises entre Zurich et les Grisons s'effectuait encore par étapes en bateau, Weesen était un port important.

Veduta di **Weesen**, all'estremità occidentale del Walensee (Canton San Gallo). All'epoca in cui su alcuni tratti i trasporti di merci fra Zurigo e i Grigioni avvenivano ancora con i battelli, Weesen era un porto importante.

Looking down on **Weesen** at the western end of the Walensee in the Canton of St. Gallen. Weesen was a flourishing port in the days when goods were transported mostly by water between Zurich and the Grisons.

Ein an Herbsttagen übliches Bild: Nebelmeer über dem **Tal der Linth** im Kanton Glarus, darüber Mürtschenstock, Fronalpstock und Schilt. Mit seinen 2441 m Höhe bildet der Mürtschenstock einen markanten Eckpfeiler am Eingang zum Glarnerland.

Une image courante les jours d'automne: mer de brouillard sur la **vallée de Linth**, canton de Glaris, surplombée des Mürtschenstock, Fronalpstock et Schilt. Culminant à 2441 m, le Mürtschenstock se dresse comme un monumental pilier à l'entrée du pays de Glaris.

Uno spettacolo usuale nei giorni autunnali: un mare di nebbia ricopre la **valle della Linth** nel Canton Glarona. Al di sopra della nebbia ci sono il Mürtschenstock, il Fronalpstock e lo Schilt. Con i suoi 2441 m di altezza, il Mürtschenstock costituisce un imponente pilastro all'ingresso della regione glaronese.

A scene that is not unusual on autumn days: a sea of cloud fills the **Linth Valley** in the Canton of Glarus. Above it rise the mountains: Mürtschenstock, Fronalpstock and Schilt. The Mürtschenstock, 2441 metres high, stands like a huge sentinel at the entrance to the valleys of Glarus.

Graubünden · Grisons · Grigioni

1 **2** **3** **4** **5**

Chur, die Hauptstadt des Kantons Graubünden, ist seit dem 4. Jhdt. Bischofssitz. In der Bildmitte, an den bischöflichen Hof anschliessend, die spätromanische Kathedrale St. Maria Himmelfahrt, rechts die ehemalige Klosterkirche St. Luzius.

Coire, chef-lieu du canton des Grisons, est siège épiscopal depuis le 4ème siècle. Au centre, contiguë à la cour de l'évêché, la cathédrale St. Maria Himmelfahrt, roman tardif, à droite l'ancienne église abbatiale de St. Luzius.

Coira, capitale dei Grigioni, è sede vescovile fin dal 4. sec. Al centro, adiacente al vescovado, si nota la cattedrale tardo-romanica di St. Maria Himmelfahrt, a destra la chiesa conventuale di St. Luzius.

Chur, the capital of the Canton of the Grisons, has been a bishop's see since the 4th century. At the centre of this picture is the Late Romanesque cathedral of the Assumption adjoining the episcopal palace; on the right is the church of St.Lucius.

Die Gegend um den **Prätschlisee** ist nur eines der vielen Wanderziele, die im Umkreis von Arosa liegen. Der Sommer- und Winterkurort liegt auf 1775 m.ü.M. und ist von Chur aus mit der Rhätischen Bahn oder über eine kurvenreiche Strasse erreichbar.

La région autour du **Prätschlisee** n'est que l'un des nombreux buts d'excursion dans les environs d'Arosa. La station d'été et d'hiver est située à 1774 m d'altitude et peut être atteinte depuis Coire par les chemins de fer rhétiques ou une route sinueuse.

La regione intorno al **Prätschlisee** è solo una delle tante mete che gli escursionisti trovano intorno ad Arosa. Questa stazione climatica invernale ed estiva è a 1775 m.s.m. e si può raggiungere da Coira con le Ferrovie retiche o con una strada ricca di curve.

The country around the **Prätschlisee**, a small mountain lake, is only one of the settings frequented by walkers in Arosa. This summer and winter resort, at an altitude of 1775 metres, can be reached from Chur by the Rhaetian Railway or up a winding road.

Was die Nordsee als braune Brühe erreicht, ist hier noch klar und sauber: Der **Glenner** (Glogn) vereinigt die Bäche des Valsertales und des Lugnez und mündet bei Ilanz in den Vorderrhein.

Les eaux qui parviendront à la mer du Nord sous forme de boue brunâtre sont encore claires et propres ici: le **Glenner** réunit les rivières de la vallée de Vals et du Lugnez et se jette vers Ilanz dans le Rhin antérieur.

L'acqua che arriva poi al Mare del Nord in forma di brodaglia marrone, qui è ancora limpida e pulita: il **Glenner** (Glogn) raccoglie i torrenti della valle di Vals e di Lugnez e a Ilanz si getta nel Reno anteriore.

Waters that are a brown soup when they reach the North Sea are here still crystal clear: the **Glenner** (Romansh Glogn) collects the streams of the valleys of Vals and Lugnez and flows into the Vorderrhein near Ilanz.

Serneus in der Talschaft des Prättigaus, an der Strecke Landquart - Klosters - Davos. Das Dorf liegt etwas abseits von Bahn und Strasse und konnte sich seinen ursprünglichen Charakter bis heute weitgehend erhalten.

Serneus, dans la vallée du Prättigau, sur le trajet Landquart - Klosters - Davos. Le village est situé à l'écart des chemins de fer et routes et a pu préserver dans une large mesure jusqu'à nos jours son caractère originel.

Serneus, nella valle di Prättigau, lungo la strada Landquart - Klosters - Davos. Il villaggio è leggermente discosto dalla strada e dalla ferrovia ed ha potuto conservare fino ad oggi il suo carattere originario.

The village of **Serneus** in the Prättigau, the valley leading up from Landquart to Klosters, lies a little way off the road and railway line and has been able to conserve most of its pristine character.

Der Höhenkurort **Seewis** (947 m ü. M.) geniesst dank seiner südseitigen Hanglage über dem Prättigau ein recht mildes Klima. Im Hintergrund ist der Gipfel der Schesaplana zu erkennen, die mit fast 3000 m Höhe die markanteste Erhebung der Rätikon-Kette bildet.

La station d'altitude **Seewis** (947 m) jouit, grâce à sa situation sur un versant sud au-dessus du Prättigau, d'un climat assez doux. En arrière-plan, on reconnaît le sommet de la Schesaplana qui, avec une altitude de près de 3000 m, domine la chaîne de Rätikon.

Grazie alla sua posizione su un pendio rivolto a sud, la stazione climatica alpina **Seewis** (947 m.s.m.) gode di un clima molto mite. Sullo sfondo si nota la vetta della Schesaplana, che con quasi 3000 m di altezza costituisce la cima più elevata della catena del Rätikon.

The resort of **Seewis** (947 metres) is located on a southern slope above the Prättigau and has a comparatively mild climate. To the rear is the Schesaplana summit, nearly 3000 metres high and the most striking feature of the Rätikon Chain.

1

2

3

4

St. Moritz (romanisch San Murezzan), 1822 m ü. M., ist einer der renommiertesten Sommer- und Winterkurorte des gesamten Alpenraumes. Wahrzeichen des Dorfes sind der "Schiefe Turm" (um 1500 erbaut), das Segantini-Museum und die weltbekannten Hotels Palace (mit Turm) und Kulm (dahinter). Am südlichen Ende des St. Moritzersees liegt St. Moritz Bad, dessen eisenhaltige Heilquellen seit Jahrhunderten bekannt sind.

St. Moritz (en romanche San Murezzan), 1822 m, est l'une des stations d'été et d'hiver les plus renommées dans l'ensemble de la région des Alpes. La "tour penchée" (construite vers 1500), le musée Segantini et l'hôtel Palace mondialement connu (avec tour) ainsi que Kulm (à l'arrière) sont les principaux symboles du village. St. Moritz Bad, dont les sources curatives ferrugineuses sont connues depuis des siècles, est situé à l'extrémité sud du lac de St. Moritz.

St. Moritz (in romancio San Murezzan), 1822 m.s.m., è una delle stazioni turistiche estive ed invernali più conosciute di tutte le Alpi. Simboli del paese sono la "Torre pendente" (costruita intorno al 1500), il Museo Segantini e gli alberghi di fama mondiale Palace (con la torre) e Kulm (dietro). All'estremità meridionale del Lago di St. Moritz si trova St. Moritz Bad, le cui fonti termali ricche di ferro sono conosciute da secoli.

St. Moritz (Romansh San Murezzan), 1822 metres, is one of the most famous summer and winter resorts in the Alps. Conspicuous buildings are the "Leaning Tower" (built about 1500), the Segantini Museum and the prestigious hotels Palace (with tower) and Kulm (behind it). At the southern end of the lake lies St. Moritz Bad, with chalybeate medicinal springs that have been known for centuries.

Die spätromanische Saalkirche St. Lorenz in **Sils-Maria**. Das Dorf (romanisch Segl) mit den beiden Ortsteilen Maria und Baselgia liegt auf der Ebene zwischen dem Silvaplaner- und dem Silsersee.

L'église de St. Lorenz à une nef, roman tardif, à **Sils-Maria**. Le village (en romanche Segl), avec ses deux zones Maria et Baselgia, est situé sur la plaine entre le lac de Silvaplana et le Silsersee.

La chiesa tardo-romanica di St. Lorenz, a **Sils-Maria**. Il paese (in romancio Segl), con le due frazioni di Maria e Baselgia, è situato nel piano fra il Lago di Silvaplana e quello di Sils.

The Late Romanesque hall-type church of St. Lorenz in **Sils-Maria** (Romansh Segl). The village lies in the plain between the lakes of Silvaplana and Sils and is divided into two parts, Maria and Baselgia.

Die auf rund 1800 m gelegene Talschaft des Oberengadins verdankt ihr einzigartiges Landschaftsbild den zwischen hohen Bergketten eingebetteten Seen. In Blickrichtung zum Malojapass liegen der **Silvaplanersee** und der **Silsersee**.

La vallée de la Haute-Engadine, à quelque 1800 m d'altitude, doit son paysage unique aux deux lacs nichés entre de hautes chaînes montagneuses. Les **lacs de Silvaplana** et **Sils** se situent dans la perspective vers le col de la Maloja.

La vallata dell'Alta Engadina, a 1800 m di altitudine, deve i suoi eccezionali panorami ai laghetti incastonati fra le alte catene montagnose. Guardando in direzione del Passo del Maloja, troviamo il **Lago di Silvaplana** e il **Lago di Sils**.

The Valley of the Upper Engadine, situated at an altitude of some 1800 metres, owes much of its unique scenic charm to lakes flanked by high mountain chains. The **Lakes of Silvaplana** and **Sils** lie on the way up to the Maloja Pass.

Morgenstimmung bei **Silvaplana**. Hier beginnt der Julierpass, der das Engadin mit dem Domleschg und dem Bündner Rheintal verbindet. Im Hintergrund sind die Masten der Corvatsch-Schwebebahn zu erkennen, die auf eine Höhe von 3295 m ü. M. führt.

Ambiance de crépuscule sur **Silvaplana**. C'est ici que débute le col de Julier qui relie l'Engadine avec le Domleschg et la vallée du Rhin dans les Grisons. A l'arrière-plan, on reconnaît les mâts du téléphérique de la Corvatsch qui conduit à une altitude de 3295m.

Atmosfera mattutina a **Silvaplana**. Qui inizia il passo dello Julier, che collega l'Engadina con il Domleschg e la valle del Reno nei Grigioni. Sullo sfondo si possono notare i piloni della funivia del Corvatsch, che porta ad un'altitudine di 3295 m.s.m.

Morning over **Silvaplana**. The road over the Julier Pass, which connects the Engadine with the Domleschg and the Rhine Valley, starts here. In the background the pylons of the Corvatsch aerial cableway are visible; it transports passengers to an altitude of 3295 metres.

1

2

3

4

5

Das **Morteratschtal** bei Pontresina wird von einem gewaltigen Riegel abgeschlossen, der durch den Morteratschgletscher und die Berninagruppe (4049 m ü. M.) gebildet wird. Diese Gebirgswelt ist bei Bergwanderern und Hochgebirgstouristen sehr beliebt.

La **vallée de Morteratsch** vers Pontresina est fermée par un puissant verrou formé par le glacier de Morteratsch et le groupe de la Bernina (4049 m). Ce massif est très apprécié des randonneurs et touristes de haute montagne.

La **Valle di Morteratsch**, vicino a Pontresina, viene chiusa da una gigantesca barriera formata dal ghiacciaio del Morteratsch e dal gruppo del Bernina (4049 m.s.m.). Questa regione alpina è molto apprezzata da escursionisti e turisti di alta montagna.

The **Morteratsch Valley** near Pontresina ends before the imposing barrier formed by the Bernina group (4049 metres) and the Morteratsch Glacier. These mountains are much loved by alpinists and mountain hikers.

Ausserhalb des Kurortes Celerina liegt die romanische Saalkirche **San Gian**. Der Chor und der kleine Turm links stammen aus dem 11., der grosse Campanile aus dem 17. Jhdt. Wandmalereien aus dem 15. Jhdt. sind teilweise noch erhalten.

L'église romane à une nef de **San Gian** est située à l'extérieur de la station de Celerina. Le choeur et la petite tour à gauche datent du 11ème siècle, le grand campanile du 17ème siècle. Des peintures murales du 15ème siècle sont encore partiellement conservées.

Poco fuori della rinomata stazione climatica di Celerina si trova la chiesa romanica di **San Gian**. Il coro e la torretta a sinistra risalgono all'11. sec., il grande campanile al 17. sec. In parte si sono conservati degli affreschi del 15. sec.

The Romanesque hall-type church of **San Gian** stands just outside the resort of Celerina. The chancel and the small tower on the left date from the 11th century, the big campanile from the 17th. There are partly preserved frescoes from the 15th century.

Flusslandschaft am **Inn** bei Zuoz. Der Rauhreif einer kalten, kristallklaren Nacht hat Bäume und Sträucher überzogen und damit eine typische Engadiner Winterstimmung geschaffen.

Paysage fluvial au bord de l'**Inn** vers Zuoz. Le givre d'une nuit froide et claire a revêtu les arbres et broussailles, créant une ambiance hivernale typique à l'Engadine.

Paesaggio fluviale lungo l'**Inn**, a Zuoz. La brina di una notte fredda e cristallina ha ricoperto alberi e cespugli, creando un'atmosfera invernale tipica dell'Engadina.

A river landscape beside the **Inn** near Zuoz. The frost of a crystal-clear night has left its white veil over trees and shrubs, creating the typical magic of winter in the Engadine.

Spätherbstliche Aussicht beim Unterengadiner Dorf **Ftan**, das auf einem etwas erhöhten Plateau über dem Talgrund liegt. Während die Lärchennadeln gelb geworden sind, hat der erste Schnee die oberhalb der Waldgrenze liegenden Bergflanken bereits überzuckert.

Vue de fin d'automne vers le village de Basse-Engadine **Ftan**, situé sur un plateau légèrement surélevé au-dessus du fond de la vallée. Pendant que les aiguilles des mélèzes ont jauni, la première neige a revêtu les flancs de montagne situés au-dessus de la limite des forêts.

Una veduta di tardo autunno del paese di **Ftan**, Bassa Engadina, che sorge su un piccolo altipiano, sopra al fondovalle. Mentre gli aghi dei larici sono ingialliti, sopra al limite del bosco, la prima neve ha già imbiancato i pendii delle montagne.

Late autumn over the Lower Engadine village of **Ftan**, which stands on a small plateau above the valley bed. The needles of the larches have turned yellow, and a first scattering of snow lies on the flanks of the mountains above the tree line.

Das schmale Tal des Unterengadins wurde jahrhundertelang durch das trutzige **Schloss Tarasp** bewacht. Heute beherbergt die über dem Kurort Schuls Tarasp Vulpera liegende Schlossanlage aus dem 11. bis 17. Jhdt. ein Museum.

L'étroite vallée de Basse-Engadine a été gardée pendant des siècles par le **château fort de Tarasp**. Aujourd'hui, ce château situé au-dessus de la station de Scuol Tarasp Vulpera et construit entre le 11ème et le 17ème siècle abrite un musée.

L'angusta valle della Bassa Engadina ha potuto contare per secoli sulla vigilanza del severo **castello di Tarasp**, costruito fra l'11. e il 17. sec. Oggigiorno la roccaforte, che domina sulla stazione climatica di Tarasp Vulpera, ospita un museo.

The narrow valley of the Lower Engadine was watched over for centuries by the formidable **Tarasp Castle**. Today a museum is housed in this fortress, built between the 11th and 17th centuries, that towers above the resort of Scuol Tarasp Vulpera.

Wallis · Valais · Vallese

1·5

1

2

3

4

5

Wenn es einen Berg gibt, der zu einem unverwechselbaren Symbol für die Schweiz wurde, so ist es das **Matterhorn** (4478 m ü. M.). Die einzigartige Pyramidenform machte den Zermatter Hausberg zu einem der berühmtesten und meistfotografierten Gipfel der Welt.

S'il est un sommet qui est devenu un symbole incomparable de la Suisse, c'est bien le **Cervin** (4478 m). Sa forme pyramidale unique a fait de la montagne de Zermatt l'un des plus célèbres sommets du monde, et aussi l'un des plus photographiés.

Se c'è una montagna che è divenuta simbolo inconfondibile della Svizzera, questa è senz'altro il **Cervino** (4478 m.s.m.). L'eccezionale forma piramidale ha fatto della montagna di Zermatt la vetta più famosa e più fotografata del mondo.

If there is a mountain that has become a symbol of Switzerland, it is the **Matterhorn** (4478 metres). Its unique steep, pyramidal outline has made Zermatt's doorstep mountain one of the most famous and most frequently photographed summits in the world.

Erst eine Luftaufnahme vermag die grandiose Stellung des **Matterhorns** zu veranschaulichen. Die Pyramide steht fast vollständig isoliert inmitten eines gewaltigen Eispanzers (rechts im Bild der Zmuttgletscher).

Seule une photo prise d'avion peut restituer la position grandiose du **Cervin**. La pyramide est presque entièrement isolée au centre d'une impressionnante carapace de glace (à droite, le glacier de Zmutt).

Solo con una fotografia aerea ci si può render conto della posizione grandiosa del **Cervino**. La piramide si trova quasi completamente isolata, al centro di un'enorme corazza di ghiaccio (a destra, nella foto, il ghiacciaio dello Zmutt).

A bird's-eye view brings out the full grandeur of the **Matterhorn**. It stands in isolation amidst seas of glacier ice (on the right the Zmutt Glacier).

Im Sommer wird das "Horu" jeweils von Alpinisten aus aller Welt bestiegen, wobei der **Hörnligrat** (Mitte) die bevorzugte Route darstellt. Zum Anlass des 125jährigen Jubiläums der Erstbesteigung erklomm im Sommer 1990 unter anderen ein 91-jähriger Bergführer den prestigeträchtigen Gipfel.

En été, le "Horu" est la cible des alpinistes du monde entier et le **Hörnligrat** (au centre) la route préférée. A l'occasion du 125ème anniversaire de la première ascension, un guide âgé de 91 ans a été l'un des alpinistes à gravir ce sommet prestigieux.

In estate l'"Horu" viene scalato da alpinisti di tutto il mondo. La via preferita è l'**Hörnligrat** (al centro). In occasione del 125. centenario della prima scalata, nell'estate 1990, anche una guida alpina novantunenne ha voluto salire sulla prestigiosa vetta.

In summer the "Horu", as the locals call it, is scaled by climbers from all over the world, the preferred route being the **Hörnligrat** (centre). In summer 1990 a ninety-one-year-old guide climbed the prestigious peak to celebrate the 125th anniversary of the first ascent.

Die Erstbesteigung des Matterhorns bildete den Grundstein der beispielhaften touristischen Karriere von **Zermatt**. Die prachtvolle Lage am Fusse des berühmten Berges verhalf dem Ort zu Weltruhm - trotzdem konnte der Dorfcharakter weitgehend erhalten bleiben.

La première ascension du Cervin a marqué le point de départ de l'exceptionnelle carrière touristique de **Zermatt**. Sa magnifique situation au pied de la fameuse montagne a permis au village d'atteindre une renommée mondiale - et néanmoins, le caractère villageois a pu être largement préservé.

La prima scalata del Cervino diede il via all'esemplare carriera turistica di **Zermatt**. La magnifica posizione ai piedi della montagna famosa ha permesso alla località di conquistarsi una fama mondiale.

The first ascent of the Matterhorn initiated the unparalleled rise of **Zermatt** to touristic fame. Its magnificent situation at the foot of the great mountain spread its name worldwide, yet much of the original character of the village has been preserved.

Das **Matterhorn** (links) für einmal aus einer anderen Perspektive. Zusammen mit den Gipfeln des Obergabelhorns und der Dent d'Hérens rückt es optisch zu einer imposanten Gebirgsformation zusammen.

Le **Cervin** (à gauche), pour une fois d'une autre perspective. Avec les sommets Obergabelhorn et Dent d'Hérens, il compose visuellement une imposante formation montagneuse.

Il **Cervino** (a sinistra), visto per una volta da un'altra prospettiva. Insieme con le vette dell'Obergabelhorn e del Dent d'Hérens un massiccio imponente.

The **Matterhorn** (left) seen from an unusual angle. When joined by the summits of the Obergabelhorn and the Dent d'Hérens, it makes an imposing mountain brotherhood.

Wallis · Valais · Vallese

1

2

3

4

Einen unvergesslichen Ausblick - im Sommer wie im Winter - bietet der 3131 m hohe **Gornergrat**, der von Zermatt aus bequem mit einer Zahnradbahn erreicht wird. Das eindrucksvolle Gletscher- und Gebirgs-panorama wird von lauter Viertausendern gekrönt: Von links nach rechts Monte Rosa mit Dufourspitze (4634 m ü. M., höchster Punkt der Schweiz), Liskamm, die "Zwillinge" Castor und Pollux sowie das Breithorn.

Berggipfel erheben sich gewaltig und gespenstisch aus den etwa auf gleicher Höhe schwebenden Wolken und Nebelschwaden. In der Bildmitte links das **Obergabelhorn**.

Die 4357 m hohe Felspyramide der **Dent Blanche** ("weisser Zahn") löst sich in den ersten Sonnenstrahlen aus dem Morgennebel. Der Berg ist fast vollständig von Gletschereis umschlossen.

Kurz vor Sonnenuntergang auf dem riesigen Plateau des Trientgletschers. Über dem Eis erheben sich die **Aiguilles Dorées** (3509 m ü. M.), deren steile Wände und Kanten zu anspruchsvollen Kletterpartien einladen.

Un panorama inoubliable - été comme hiver - offert à partir du **Gornergrat**, 3131 m, confortablement atteignable depuis Zermatt par un chemin de fer à crémaillère. L'impressionnante vue sur les glaciers et montagnes est couronnée par une pléthore de 4000: de gauche à droite, Mont-Rose avec pointe Dufour (4634 m, point le plus haut de la Suisse), Liskamm, les "jumeaux" Castor et Pollux ainsi que le Breithorn.

Les sommets se détachent dans une vigueur fantomatique des nuages et nappes de brume qui planent presque à même hauteur. Au centre à gauche, l'**Obergabelhorn**.

La pyramide de rocher haute de 4357 m de la **Dent Blanche** se détache de la brume matinale dans les premiers rayons du soleil. La montagne est presque entièrement entourée de glaciers.

Peu avant le coucher du soleil, sur le gigantesque plateau du glacier de Trient. Les **Aiguilles Dorées** (3509 m), dont les parois et arêtes raides invitent à d'audacieuses varappes, émergent de la glace.

Una vista indimenticabile - in estate come in inverno, viene offerta dal **Gornergrat**, comodamente raggiungibile da Zermatt con una ferrovia a cremagliera. Lo splendido panorama dei ghiacciai e delle montagne viene coronato da numerose vette superiori ai quattromila: da sinistra a destra il Monte Rosa, con la Punta Dufour (4634 m.s.m., il punto più alto della Svizzera), il Liskamm, i "gemelli" Castore e Polluce e il Breithorn.

Le vette delle montagne si ergono, grandiose e spettrali, dalle nubi e dai banchi di nebbia che arrivano quasi alla medesima altezza. Al centro, verso sinistra, si può notare l'**Obergabelhorn**.

La piramide di roccia del **Dent Blanche**, alta 4357 m, illuminata dai primi raggi di sole, sopra alla nebbia mattutina. La montagna è ricoperta quasi completamente di ghiacciai.

Poco prima del tramonto sul gigantesco piano del ghiacciaio del Trient. Al di sopra del ghiaccio si elevano le **Aiguilles Dorées** (3509 m.s.m.), con pareti e fianchi ripidissimi, che invitano ad esigenti scalate.

An unforgettable view is afforded in summer and winter by the **Gornergrat**, 3131 metres in height, which can easily be reached by rack railway from Zermatt. The majestic panorama of peaks and glaciers comprises various summits above 4000 metres high. From left to right: Monte Rosa with the Dufourspitze (4634 metres, Switzerland's highest point), Liskamm, the "twins" Castor and Pollux, and the Breithorn.

Mighty summits here rise in a ghostly choreography from the lofty oceans of cloud and mist. Left of centre is the **Obergabelhorn**.

The rocky bastion of the **Dent Blanche** ("white tooth"), 4357 metres high, emerges from the morning mists as the first rays of the sun break through. The Dent Blanche is almost wholly encircled by glaciers.

Just before sunset on the vast plateau of the Trient Glacier. Out of the ice rise the **Aiguilles Dorées** (3509 metres), with steep faces and ridges that challenge ambitious climbers.

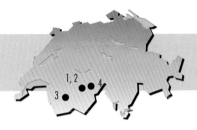

1

2

3

4

Blatten ob Naters ist eines der charakteristischen Walliser Dörfer mit Häusern aus sonnenverbranntem Holz. Die kleinen Scheunen ("Speicher") stehen zum Schutz vor Mäusen auf Pfählen und Steinplatten.

Winterstimmung im tiefverschneiten **Lötschental**. Hier haben sich viele alte Volksbräuche erhalten; die furchterregenden Lötschentaler Holzmasken sind weit herum bekannt.

Sitten, die Hauptstadt des Kantons Wallis, wird von zwei markanten Burghügeln flankiert: Links Tourbillon mit dem im 13. Jhdt. als Bischofssitz erbauten Schloss. Auf Valeria (rechts) thront ebenfalls ein Schloss (erstmals um 1050 erwähnt) sowie die Kirche Notre-Dame-de-Valère.

Welt des Eises am **Grossen Aletschgletscher**. Der mit 24 km längste Eisstrom der Schweiz bildet die grösste zusammenhängende Gletscherfläche der europäischen Alpen.
Um diesen einzigartigen Blick über die gigantische Gletscherwelt geniessen zu können, braucht es keine alpinistischen Kenntnisse: Von Mörel oberhalb Brig führt eine Schwebebahn auf die Riederalp, von wo diese Stelle in einem 45minütigen Fussmarsch zu erreichen ist.

Blatten, au-dessus de Naters, est l'un des villages valaisans les plus caractéristiques avec ses maisons en bois brûlé par le soleil. Les petits mazots ("Speicher") sont posés sur des pilotis et plaques de pierre, comme protection contre les souris.

Ambiance hivernale au **Lötschental** enfoui sous la neige. Ici, de nombreuses coutumes populaires ancestrales ont survécu; les effrayants masques en bois sont connus loin à la ronde.

Sion, chef-lieu du canton du Valais, est dominé par deux collines: à gauche, Tourbillon, avec son château construit au 13ème siècle comme siège épiscopal. Un château (mentionné pour la première fois en 1050), trône aussi sur Valère (à droite), ainsi que l'église Notre-Dame-de-Valère.

Univers de la glace, sur le **grand glacier de l'Aletsch**. La plus longue rivière de glace de Suisse, 24 km, forme la plus grande surface de glacier d'un seul tenant des Alpes européennes.
Pour savourer ce panorama unique sur l'univers gigantesque du glacier, il n'est pas nécessaire d'être un bon alpiniste: un téléphérique conduit de Mörel au-dessus de Brigue sur la Riederalp, d'où cet emplacement peut être atteint par une promenade à pied de 45 minutes.

Blatten sopra Naters, è uno dei caratteristici paesi del Vallese, con case di legno bruciate dal sole. I piccoli fienili ("Speicher") sono costruiti su pali e lastre di pietra, per proteggerli dai topi.

Atmosfera invernale nella **Lötschental**, ricoperta da una spessa coltre di neve. Qui vigono ancora oggi numerose antiche usanze. Da qui provengono le note maschere di legno, dai volti che vogliono incutere paura.

Sion, la capitale del Vallese, è fiancheggiata da due massicce colline fortificate: a sinistra Tourbillon, con il castello costruito nel 13. sec. come vescovado. Su Valeria (a destra) troneggiano pure un castello (menzionato per la prima volta nel 1050) nonché la chiesa di Notre-Dame-de-Valère.

Il grande ghiacciaio dell'Aletsch è un mondo di ghiaccio. La fiumana gelata, con 24 km la più lunga della Svizzera, costituisce il ghiacciaio con la maggior superficie unita di tutte le Alpi.
Per poter godere della vista eccezionale di questo gigantesco mondo di ghiaccio, non bisogna essere grandi alpinisti: da Mörel, sopra a Briga, una funivia porta fino a Riederalp, da dove si può raggiungere il sentiero panoramico con una marcia a piedi di 45 minuti.

Blatten above Naters is a characteristic Valaisan village with houses of sun-darkened timber. The small storage barns are raised on supports topped with stone slabs to protect them from rodents.

The Lötschental lies deep in winter snow. Many old customs have survived in this high valley, and the fearsome-looking masks the valley-dwellers wear on these occasions are known far and wide.

Sion, capital of the Valais, is flanked by two striking hills. On the left Tourbillon with a castle built as a bishop's seat in the 13th century; on the right Valeria with a castle (first mentioned about 1050) and the church of Notre-Dame-de-Valère.

A world of ice on the **Great Aletsch Glacier**. With a length of 24 kilometres, this is not only Switzerland's longest glacier but the biggest single glaciated area in the Alps.
No qualifications in alpinism are needed to enjoy this unique view of the gigantic glacier. An aerial cableway runs from Mörel above Brig on to the Riederalp, and the photographer's station can be reached from there in a 45-minute walk.

Ticino · Tessin

1

2

3

4

5

Ascona, sulle rive del Lago Maggiore. Il clima mite, di tipo meridionale, permette la crescita di una vegetazione subtropicale. Sulla grande isola di Brissago (al centro) esiste un magnifico giardino botanico.

Bei **Ascona** am Ufer des Lago Maggiore. Das milde, südliche Klima ermöglicht eine subtropische Vegetation. Auf einer der Brissago-Inseln (in der Bildmitte) ist ein prachtvoller Botanischer Garten angelegt.

Vers **Ascona**, sur la rive du lac Majeur. Le climat doux et méridional favorise une végétation subtropicale. Un superbe jardin botanique a été aménagé sur une des îles de Brissago (au centre).

Near **Ascona** on the shores of the Lago Maggiore. Subtropical vegetation thrives in the mild climate. There is a fine Botanic Garden on the larger of the Brissago Islands (left of centre).

Su un ripido pendio sopra al Lago Maggiore troneggia il paesino di **Ronco**, con la chiesa parrocchiale di San Martino. L'edificio, con una sola navata, risale al 15. sec. e vanta un coro con preziosi affreschi e volte con stucchi meravigliosi.

An einem Steilhang über dem Lago Maggiore thront das Dörfchen **Ronco** mit der Pfarrkirche San Martino. Der einschiffige Bau aus dem 15. Jhdt. ist mit Chorfresken und grossartigen Gewölbe-Stukkaturen ausgeschmückt.

Le village de **Ronco** trône sur un flanc raide au-dessus du lac Majeur, avec son église paroissiale San Martino. La construction à une nef du 15ème siècle a un chœur orné de fresques et de somptueuses voûtes en stuc.

The little village of **Ronco** with its parish church of San Martino clings to the steep slope above the Lago Maggiore. The single-nave building from the 15th century has frescoes in the chancel and splendid stucco work in its vaults.

La chiesa della **Madonna del Sasso**, sopra a Locarno, è meta di numerosi pellegrinaggi. Nella forma attuale la costruzione risale al 16.-17. sec. All'interno si conservano dipinti e figure intagliate del 15. sec.

Die Wallfahrtskirche **Madonna del Sasso** in Orselina oberhalb Locarno wurde im 16. und 17. Jhdt. in ihrer heutigen Form erbaut. Im Innern sind Gemälde und geschnitzte Figuren aus dem 15. Jhdt. erhalten.

L'église de pèlerinage **Madonna del Sasso** à Orselina au-dessus de Locarno a été construite aux 16ème et 17ème siècles dans sa forme actuelle. A l'intérieur, des peintures et sculptures taillées du 15ème siècle ont pu être conservées.

The **Madonna del Sasso** in Orselina above Locarno is a place of pilgrimage that was built as it appears today in the 16th and 17th centuries. It possesses paintings and carvings from the 15th century.

La strada del Passo della Novena, lunga 13 km, collega l'Alto Vallese alla Leventina. Sul lato del Ticino la strada attraversa la Val Bedretto - nella foto il paesino di **Fontana**.

Die 13 km lange Nufenenpassstrasse verbindet das Oberwallis mit der Leventina. Auf der Tessiner Seite führt die Strasse durch das Bedrettotal - im Bild der Weiler **Fontana**.

La route du col du Nufenen, longue de 13 km, relie le Haut Valais à la Leventina. Du côté tessinois, la route traverse la vallée de Bedretto - sur la photo, le hameau de **Fontana**.

The road up to the Nufenen Pass is 13 kilometres long. It connects the Ticino with the Upper Valais by way of the Bedretto Valley. The little village of **Fontana** lies on the route.

Uno dei simboli della **Valle Verzasca** è il ponte di pietra di Lavertezzo, di epoca medievale. Su un tratto di pochi chilometri, la strada porta dal clima mediterraneo sul Lago Maggiore alle ripide Alpi ticinesi.

Eines der Wahrzeichen des **Verzascatals** ist die mittelalterliche Steinbrücke von Lavertezzo. Das Tal führt vom mediterranen Klima am Lago Maggiore in wenigen Kilometern zur schroffen Bergwelt der Tessiner Alpen.

Le pont en pierre médiéval de Lavertezzo est l'un des symboles de la **vallée de Verzasca**. La vallée passe en quelques kilomètres du climat méditerranéen des bords du lac Majeur à l'univers escarpé des Alpes tessinoises.

The medieval stone bridge at Lavertezzo is one of the gems of the **Verzasca Valley**. This valley, though only some 20 kilometres long, runs up from the Lago Maggiore with its Mediterranean climate to the harsh fastnesses of the Ticinese Alps.

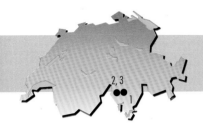

1

2

3

Sonogno si trova a 918 m.s.m. alla fine della Valle Verzasca. La strada termina qui, ma numerosi sentieri di montagna portano nelle valli vicine. Il cammino sulla Forcla di Redorta porta in Val Lavizzara, aggirando il Monte Zucchero (al centro).

Sonogno liegt auf 918 m ü. M. am Ende des Verzascatals. Während die Strasse hier zu Ende ist, führen Gebirgspfade in die benachbarten Täler. Der Weg über die Forcla di Redorta führt am Monte Zucchero (Bildmitte) vorbei ins Lavizzaratal.

Le village de **Sonogno** est situé à 918 m d'altitude à l'extrémité de la vallée de Verzasca. Si la route s'achève ici, des sentiers de montagne conduisent aux vallées latérales. Le chemin au-dessus de la Forcla di Redorta mène le long du Monte Zucchero (au centre) vers la vallée de Lavizzara.

Sonogno lies at an altitude of 918 metres at the top of the Verzasca Valley. The road ends here, but footpaths run on into the higher country. The one over the Forcla di Redorta passes Monte Zucchero (2736 metres, centre) before descending into the Valle Lavizzara.

Foroglio, un paese di contadini di montagna, è in Val Bavona, una valle laterale della Val Maggia. A causa delle carenti possibilità di guadagno, i paesi come Foroglio devono lottare con il problema dell'esodo dei giovani.

Das Bergbauerndorf **Foroglio** liegt im Val Bavona, einem Seitental des Maggiatales. Infolge mangelnder Erwerbsmöglichkeiten haben Orte wie Foroglio mit dem Problem der Abwanderung der jüngeren Generation zu kämpfen.

Le village de paysans de montagne de **Foroglio** est situé dans le Val Bavona, une vallée latérale de la vallée de la Maggia. En raison de manque de possibilités de travail, des localités telles que Foroglio ont été confrontées au problème de l'exode des jeunes.

The farming village of **Foroglio** lies in the Val Bavona, a side valley of the Maggia. There are few jobs to be had up here, so that villages such as Foroglio have to face the problem of the exodus of the younger generation.

La Val Maggia è probabilmente la più conosciuta fra le valli ticinesi. Nella foto il paese di **Cevio**, con la chiesa di Santa Maria Assunta e San Giovanni. La chiesa viene citata per la prima volta nel 1252 e fu completamente ricostruita nel 16. sec.

Das Maggiatal ist das wohl bekannteste der Tessiner Bergtäler. Im Bild das Dorf **Cevio** mit der Kirche Santa Maria Assunta e San Giovanni. Das Gotteshaus wurde 1252 erstmals erwähnt und im 16. Jhdt. neu gebaut.

La vallée de la Maggia est sans doute la plus célèbre vallée d'altitude du Tessin. Sur l'illustration, le village de **Cevio** avec l'église Santa Maria Assunta e San Giovanni. Ce lieu saint est mentionné pour la première fois en 1252 et a été reconstruit au 16ème siècle.

The Valle Maggia is perhaps the best known of the lateral valleys of the Ticino. The village of **Cevio** is shown here with the church of Santa Maria Assunta e San Giovanni. First mentioned in 1252, the church was rebuilt in the 16th century.

1-4

1

2

3

4

Morcote sul Lago di Lugano. La maggior parte degli edifici con le loro caratteristiche arcate risale al 15. sec. In alto si staglia la chiesa di Santa Maria del Sasso (1462), con il famoso cimitero terrazzato.

Morcote am Luganersee. Die meisten dieser Gebäude mit ihren charakteristischen Arkaden stammen aus dem 15. Jhdt. Über dem Ort die Kirche Santa Maria del Sasso (1462) mit dem berühmten terrassierten Friedhof.

Morcote, au bord du lac de Lugano. La plupart de ces constructions, avec leurs arcades caractéristiques, datent du 15ème siècle. Surplombant le village, l'église Santa Maria del Sasso (1462) avec le célèbre cimetière en terrasses.

Morcote on the Lake of Lugano. Most of the buildings along the shore, with their characteristic arcades, were built in the 15th century. Above the village stands the church of Santa Maria del Sasso (1462) with its famous terraced cemetery.

In una delle numerose insenature del Lago di Lugano, in mezzo ad un grazioso paesaggio con un clima particolarmente mite, si trova **Agno**. Grazie all'aeroporto di Lugano-Agno il nome del paese ha acquistato rinomanza internazionale.

In der besonders milden, landschaftlich sehr reizvollen Tessiner Seenlandschaft liegt in einer der vielen Buchten des Luganersees die Ortschaft **Agno**. Dank dem Flugplatz Lugano-Agno ist der Name des Dorfes auch zu einem international bekannten Begriff geworden.

Le village d'**Agno** est situé dans l'une des nombreuses baies du lac de Lugano, dans la région des lacs tessinois au climat particulièrement doux et aux paysages pittoresques.
L'aéroport de Lugano-Agno a fait connaître le nom de ce village.

The village of **Agno** lies on one of the many bays of the Lake of Lugano. The climate here is very mild, and the lakes are famous for their scenic beauty. Agno has become known internationally because the Lugano-Agno airport is close by.

Gandria, il romantico paese di pescatori, perfettamente conservato, sembra quasi "incollato" sulla sponda rocciosa del Lago di Lugano. Vi si può arrivare da Lugano in auto o in battello, come pure a piedi, su un lungolago con una magnifica vista.

Wie an die Felsen "geklebt" wirkt das romantische, sehr gut erhaltene Fischerdorf **Gandria** am Luganersee. Es ist von Lugano aus per Schiff und Auto, aber auch zu Fuss auf einem aussichtsreichen Seeuferweg, zu erreichen.

Comme "collé" sur les falaises, tel est l'effet produit par **Gandria**, ce romantique village de pêcheurs bien conservé, niché au bord du lac de Lugano. Il est atteignable depuis Lugano par bateau ou en voiture, mais aussi à pied par un sentier longeant le lac.

The well-preserved fishing village of **Gandria** clings romantically to the rocks above the waters of the Lake of Lugano. It can be reached from Lugano either by car or boat, or else on foot along a lakeside path offering unsurpassed scenery.

Il mare di luci degli alberghi e degli eleganti negozi delle notti di **Lugano**. Sul golfo del Lago di Lugano domina l'imponente San Salvatore, alla cui vetta rocciosa (912 m) si può arrivare con una ripida funivia (fino al 60% di pendenza!) che risale al 1890. Anche se non è la capitale del Canton Ticino, Lugano è comunque l'incontestata metropoli commerciale della Svizzera italiana. Numerosi monumenti ed esposizioni sottolineano anche l'importanza culturale e storica della città.

Das Lichtermeer der Hotels und eleganten Geschäfte von **Lugano** bei Nacht. Die halbkreisförmige Bucht des Luganersees wird überragt vom markanten, schroffen San Salvatore. Auf seinen 912 m hohen Felsgipfel führt eine steile (bis 60%!) Standseilbahn aus dem Jahre 1890. Obwohl nicht die Hauptstadt des Kantons Tessin, ist Lugano doch unbestritten die geschäftliche Metropole der Südschweiz. Zahlreiche bedeutende Sehenswürdigkeiten unterstreichen auch die kulturelle und historische Bedeutung der Stadt.

L'océan de lumières des hôtels et des élégants magasins de **Lugano** by night. La baie semicirculaire du lac de Lugano est surplombée de la saillie marquante et escarpée du San Salvatore. Un funiculaire très raide (jusqu'à 60%!) qui date de 1890 mène à son sommet rocheux culminant à 912 m. Même si elle n'est pas la capitale du Tessin, Lugano est incontestablement la métropole commerciale du Sud de la Suisse. De multiples curiosités de renom soulignent encore la portée culturelle et historique de cette cité.

A sea of light from **Lugano's** hotels and fashionable stores. Above the semicircular lake bay on which the town is situated rises the abrupt eminence of the Monte San Salvatore. A steep funicular built in 1890 (with a gradient of up to 3 in 5!) runs up to its summit at 912 metres. Though not the capital of the Canton of the Ticino, Lugano is its undisputed business metropolis. Its numerous sights bear witness to its cultural and historical importance.

Bildnachweis
Source des illustrations
Fonti fotografiche
Index of photographers

Titel/titre/copertina/title
Matterhorn/Cervin/Cervino — Sigi Stangier

Innentitel/titre intérieur/copertina interna/inside title
Matterhorn/Cervin/Cervino — Sigi Stangier

Bern/Berne/Berna
Bern — Herbert Haltmeier
Berner Altstadt — Siegfried Eigstler
Emmental — Siegfried Eigstler
St. Petersinsel — Siegfried Eigstler
Twann — Herbert Haltmeier

**Berner Oberland/Oberland bernois/Oberland bernese
Bernese Oberland**
Schloss Thun — Siegfried Eigstler
Brienzer Rothorn — Herbert Haltmeier
Brienz — Siegfried Eigstler
Wetterhorn — Herbert Haltmeier
Schreckhorn und Finsteraarhorn — Herbert Haltmeier
Öschinensee — Siegfried Eigstler
Eiger, Mönch und Jungfrau — Herbert Haltmeier
Jungfraujoch — Siegfried Eigstler
Jungfraufirn — Herbert Haltmeier

**Zentralschweiz/Suisse centrale/Svizzera centrale/Central
Switzerland**
Luzern — Herbert Haltmeier
Mythen — Christian Thoma
Urnersee — Siegfried Eigstler
Turner — Hanspeter Reinhard
Fluebrig-Kette — Hanspeter Reinhard
Stansstad — Arnold Odermatt
Lungernsee — Siegfried Eigstler
Stanserhorn — Arnold Odermatt

Zug — Herbert Haltmeier
Fünffingerstöcke — Herbert Haltmeier
Oberalp-Pass — Hanspeter Reinhard

**Region lémanique/Genfersee-Region/Regione del Lemano/
Lake of Geneva region/Vaud**
Genève — Herbert Haltmeier
Jet d'Eau — Siegfried Eigstler
Lac Léman — Jacques Straesslé
Château d'Aigle — Herbert Haltmeier
Château de Chillon — Herbert Haltmeier
Lausanne — Jacques Straesslé
Vallée de Joux — Jacques Straesslé

Fribourg/Freiburg/Friborgo/Neuchâtel/Neuenburg
Fribourg/Freiburg — Herbert Haltmeier
Gruyères — Siegfried Eigstler
Font — Herbert Haltmeier
Neuchâtel — Siegfried Eigstler
Auvernier — Siegfried Eigstler

Jura/Giura
Porrentruy — Herbert Haltmeier
Lac des Brenets — Siegfried Eigstler
La Bosse — Siegfried Eigstler

**Nordwestschweiz/Nord-ouest de la Suisse/
Svizzera nord-occidentale/Northwestern Switzerland**
Basel — Herbert Haltmeier
Basler Rheinhafen — Siegfried Eigstler
Belchen — Siegfried Eigstler
Solothurn — Herbert Haltmeier
Hallwilersee — Herbert Haltmeier
Baden — Herbert Haltmeier
Bremgarten — Herbert Haltmeier

Zürich/Zurich/Zurigo
Zürich — Siegfried Eigstler
„Zur Schipfe" — Herbert Haltmeier
Regensberg — Siegfried Eigstler
Rheinau — Siegfried Eigstler

**Ostschweiz/Suisse orientale/Svizzera orientale/Eastern
Switzerland**
Munot — Herbert Haltmeier
Rheinfall — Herbert Haltmeier
Schloss Hagenwil — Herbert Haltmeier
Bodensee — Herbert Haltmeier
St. Gallen — Herbert Haltmeier
Appenzellerland — Herbert Haltmeier
Heiden — Herbert Haltmeier
Gais — Herbert Haltmeier
Werdenberg — Herbert Haltmeier
Rapperswil — Herbert Haltmeier
Weesen — Herbert Haltmeier
Tal der Linth — Hanspeter Reinhard

Graubünden/Grisons/Grigioni
Chur — Herbert Haltmeier
Prätschlisee — Herbert Haltmeier
Glenner — Siegfried Eigstler
Serneus — Siegfried Eigstler
Seewis — Herbert Haltmeier

Engadin/Engadine/Engadina/Engadine
St. Moritz — Herbert Haltmeier
Sils-Maria — Lisa Gensetter
Silvaplanersee/Silsersee — Lisa Gensetter
Silvaplana — Herbert Haltmeier
Morteratschtal — Herbert Haltmeier
San Gian — Herbert Haltmeier

Inn — Lisa Gensetter
Ftan — Lisa Gensetter
Schloss Tarasp — Christian Thoma

Wallis/Valais/Vallese
Matterhorn — Siegfried Eigstler
Matterhorn mit Zmuttgletscher — Herbert Haltmeier
Hörnligrat — Sigi Stangier
Zermatt — Siegfried Eigstler
Matterhorn — Hanspeter Reinhard
Gornergrat — Herbert Haltmeier
Obergabelhorn — Hanspeter Reinhard
Dent Blanche — Hanspeter Reinhard
Aiguilles Dorées — Hanspeter Reinhard
Blatten — Lisa Gensetter
Lötschental — Siegfried Eigstler
Sitten/Sion — Lisa Gensetter
Grosser Aletschgletscher — Siegfried Eigstler

Ticino/Tessin
Ascona — Herbert Haltmeier
Ronco — Arnold Odermatt
Madonna del Sasso — Arnold Odermatt
Fontana — Hanspeter Reinhard
Valle Verzasca — Herbert Haltmeier
Sonogno — Herbert Haltmeier
Foroglio — Lisa Gensetter
Cevio — Siegfried Eigstler
Morcote — Herbert Haltmeier
Agno — Herbert Haltmeier
Gandria — Herbert Haltmeier
Lugano — Herbert Haltmeier